MW00830968

Schaumburg Township District Library
130 South Roselle Road
Schaumburg, IL 60193

Ohhlicious, Over 70 Vegan Recipes that are Good for the Soul. Your Soul's Food.

Copyright © 2017, Michelle Grandy

All rights reserved worldwide.

No part of this book may be used or reproduced in any manner without written permission. This publication is protected under the US Copyright Act of 1976 and all other applicable international, federal, state and local laws, and all rights are reserved, including resale rights.

Ohh Michelle, LLC

Michelle Grandy

Publisher

3 Normandy Circle

Bluffton, SC 29910

www.ohhliciousfood.com/thebook

michelle@ohhmichelle.com

ISBN: 978-0692854532

Book Cover: Multi-Images Graphics

CONTENTS

INTRODUCTION 8

OHH COLLARDS! 10

CURRY CHICKPEAS & SEASONED ROASTED VEGETABLES14

QUINOA SWEET POTATO CHICKPEA BURGERS 18

BLACK-EYED PEAS AND KALE 22

WARM KALE-COLLARD SALAD 26

STIR FRY COLLARDS – OHH GREENS! 30

OHH COLORFUL BLACK BEAN, SWEET CORN, BEETS & SPINACH SALAD! 32

STUFFED MARINATED COLLARD GREENS! 38

OHH EATS… LIMA BEAN SOUP! 42

OHH EATS PESTO PASTA 46

TWO WORDS: PINTO BEANS! 50

MARINATED COLLARD GREENS 54

ARTICHOKE AND SPINACH CASSEROLE 58

SAY YES TO BRUSSELS SPROUTS & PEAS! 62

CURRY VEGETABLES - SPICES FOR THE SOUL....................64

LIMA AND COLLARDS – OHH MY! 68

BLACK-EYED PEAS WITH TURNIPS 72

STEW VEGGIES WITH COLLARDS 76

CURRY TOFU, QUINOA & VEGGIES! 80

YEP, THE PERFECT VEGAN SHEPARD'S PIE 84

SPICY CHICKPEA BURGER 88

BAKED MAC & CHEESE 92

OHHLICIOUS CHICKPEA SPINACH SALAD! 96

BOWL OF CURRY LENTIL SOUP! 98

VEGAN BURGER 102

COLD CHICKPEA SALAD 106

THE MAKINGS OF A RAW – SALAD 110

THE BEST SALAD EVER! 114

TRI COLOR CURRY BEANS – WHAT VEGANS EAT FOR DINNER 118

MARINATED KALE SALAD 120

COLORFUL BEAUTY TO MIX WITH MARINATED KALE 124

CHICKEN LENTIL SOUP 126

YES TO SIDE SALAD 130

CUCUMBER TOMATO SALAD 132

CURRY CAULIFLOWER, PINTO BEANS, FERMENTED TOFU AND TRI-COLOR QUINOA 134

SMOKED BARBECUE TEMPEH AND BLACK BEAN SLIDERS 138

ROASTED CHICKPEAS 142

MEGA GREEN SALAD 144

RED COCONUT CURRY WITH TOFU & VEGGIES 146

EGGPLANT & VEGETABLES 148

BLACK-EYED PEAS 152

VEGAN SAUCE FOR LASAGNA 156

LIGHTLY STEAMED SUPER GREENS 160

GLASS FULL OF COLLARDS & BRUSSELS SPROUTS 162

ROASTED VEGETABLES & CHICKPEAS 164

CHICKPEA & AVOCADO SANDWICH 168

HEARTY MISO SOUP 170

THE MAKING OF KALE CHIPS 174

STEW VEGGIES & TOFU WITH QUINOA 176

VEGAN CORNBREAD 180

VEGAN STEAK & CHEESE 184

MARINATED GARLIC KALE 188

AVOCADO & SPICY BLACK BEAN SOUP 192

OHH KALE YEAH! 196

GRILLED CHEESE & SPINACH – WHY NOT! 200

MARINATED COLLARDS & CHICKPEAS 202

CREAMY DILL INFUSED POTATO SALAD 206

MEGA GREEN PROTEIN 210

BIG BAD BREAKFAST 212

HEARTY BOWL OF VEGAN CHILI.................................216

OHH VEGAN CHICKEN VEGETABLE STIR-FRY! 220

TUSCAN FOREST MUSHROOMS WITH SUN DRIED TOMATOES
....224

CREAMY HUMMUS 228

CURRY LENTILS & BLUE CHIPS...................................230

OHH MY... CAULIFLOWER RICE..................................234

YES TO EDAMAME DUMPLINGS! 236

GARLIC SPINACH, SAUTEED.......................................240

VEGEN CHICKEN NOODLE SOUP................................242

GINGER LEMON APPLE PINEAPPLE BLAST 246

THE SALAD 248

TOFU SCRAMBLE TACOS 252

VEGAN MAC & CHEESE – OHH SO GOOD!..................258

CORN AND TOMATO BRUSCHETTA 262

AVOCADO TOAST...266

This book is dedicated in loving memory to my grandmother, Gussie Jackson, my teacher and best friend.

INTRODUCTION

Michelle Grandy is a byword for living what she speaks because for more than 8 years she made it her business to make people feel loved and cared for through food and lifestyle choices. She has been successful in this because her efforts come from her heart. She truly cares about the wellbeing of others. They feel it and most of them return again and again listening in to what she has to say through her food and inspiring words.

A big part of her caring is in the food. She doesn't just feed people; she nourishes them with inspiration and motivation that moves the soul. She prepares every meal and every dish as a way to contribute to the heath, well-being and vitality of others. Her food is made with love. This book is filled with healing plant based recipes from dishes prepared by Michelle over the last eight years, all motivated by her Grandmother Gussie's love and her fervent wish to help you live well and long.

And because her concept is to change the way you think about food, which has expanded over the years to encompass a healthy lifestyle, she has come to insist that the food she cooks be not only good for your body, but also good for your soul and the reason she calls these recipes your soul's food.

To that end, Michelle shares with you her very 1st Vegan Cookbook. Please enjoy these recipes and cook with love!

OHH COLLARDS!

MY STORY

Collard Greens has long been the "go to" greens cooked by my grandmother growing up. As a matter of fact, we ate them more than once weekly. Living in inner City housing meant we did not have a traditional garden nor yard space. However, my grandmother would barter work with community gardener friends to allow our family to grow vegetables, including collards.

I grew up watching my grandmother clean and cook collards for hours. Remember that! I mean, once the collards were cleaned, my grandmother would cook them for at least four hours. Undoubtedly, I cleaned and cooked my collards the same way and sure enough, my son watched me clean and cook

SHOPPING LIST

- 2 bunches organic Collard Greens
- 1 medium Sweet Onion
- 4 medium sized Turnips
- 3 Garlic Cloves
- 1 Vegan Chicken bouillon cube or two cups veggie broth
- Turmeric Powder
- Thyme
- Cumin Powder
- Bragg's liquid amino
- Tabasco sauce
- Rice Vinegar
- Liquid Smoke
- Grape Seed oil
- Black Ground Pepper
- Organic greens should be steamed-like with little water and cooked less than an hour

Visit Here For More

Information On An Instant

Pot: **goo.gl/rgdii4**

collards this way. I love organic collards because they become tender faster and cleaning is much easier, making collards a family vegetable we can enjoy during the busy week. Try this:

RECIPE

Servings 6 | Prep Time 15 mins | Total Time 40 mins

INGREDIENTS

- 2 bunches organic collard greens, cleaned, shredded, including stems
- 1 medium sweet onion, sliced
- 4 medium sized turnips, diced or chopped
- 3 garlic cloves
- 1 vegan bullion /chicken bouillon cube/ or two to three cups veggie broth
- 1 tsp of turmeric powder
- 1 tsp of thyme
- 1 tsp cumin powder
- 2 tbsp of Bragg's liquid amino
- 2 tbsp of Tabasco sauce (eyeball to taste) or 1 tbsp of red pepper flakes
- 2 tbsp of rice vinegar
- 2 tbsp liquid smoke
- 2 tbsp grape seed oil
- Black ground pepper to taste
- 2 cups water
- Organic greens should be steamed-like with little water and cooked less than an hour

DIRECTIONS

2 Ways to Prepare – Instructions:

Using an Instant Pot, place onions, turnips, all seasonings/spices, water and collards. Use hands to massage and integrate ingredients. Cover pot and press the steam option (10 min). Add five more minutes to cooking. Cook per Instant Pot.

Bring medium pot of boiling broth or 2 cups water. If water, then place chicken bullion and continue to boil. Place all ingredients in pot and boil for 2 minutes, and then allow simmering for one hour, stirring and tasting broth throughout. Collards will become tender. Enjoy!

CURRY CHICKPEAS & SEASONED ROASTED VEGETABLES

RECIPE

Servings 4 | Prep Time 10 | Total Time 30

INGREDIENTS

- 1 can organic garbanzo beans (chickpeas)
- 1 sweet potato, sliced
- 1 cup green peas (can be frozen)
- 1 zucchini, sliced
- 4 whole garlic cloves
- 2 tbsp extra virgin olive oil
- 1 tbsp nondairy butter
- 1 tbsp basil
- 1 tbsp cumin
- 1 tsp onion powder
- 1 tbsp red pepper flakes
- 1 tbsp thyme
- 1 tbsp chili powder
- 1 tbsp tamari sauce
- 1 tsp curry powder
- ½ tsp garam masala
- ½ ginger powder
- salt and pepper to taste

SHOPPING LIST

- 1 can organic Garbanzo Beans (Chickpeas)
- 1 Sweet Potato
- Green Peas (can be frozen)
- 1 Zucchini
- 4 whole Garlic Cloves
- Extra Virgin Olive Oil
- Non-Dairy Butter
- Basil
- Cumin
- Onion powder
- Red Pepper Flakes
- Thyme
- Chili Powder
- Tamari Sauce
- Curry Powder
- Garam Masala
- Ginger Powder
- Salt and Pepper

DIRECTIONS

Sweet Potatoes: Place sweet potatoes in a hot buttered skillet and cook for two minutes on each side. Remove from heat, cover and allow to sit until ready for seasoning

Oven to Roasted at 400 degree or Bake at 425 degree

Vegetable Spice Mix: In a small bowl, combine basil, parsley, cumin, red pepper flakes, chili powder, ½ onion powder, thyme, salt and pepper and sit aside

Place beans in a bowl and mix with curry powder, garam masala, ginger powder and other ½ onion powder and tamari sauce. Toss and set aside.

Place each vegetable into a bowl and mix with 1 tbsp spice mix and drizzle with oil.

On a large roasting pan or oven tray, place vegetables and marinated beans in a sectional space. Drizzle with additional oil, if needed. Roast for 20 minutes or until golden brown, turning once. Feel free to combine all ingredients onto one baking sheet. Breathe, Serve and Enjoy!

QUINOA SWEET POTATO CHICKPEA BURGERS

RECIPE

Servings 4 to 6 burgers | Prep Time 15 mins | Total Time 40 mins

INGREDIENTS

- 1 cup quinoa (cook per direction and use vegetable broth instead of water)
- 1 medium sweet potato
- 1 can garbanzo beans, organic, rinsed and drained
- 1 tbsp finely minced fresh ginger
- 1 tbsp garlic, minced
- ½ cup green onions, chopped small
- salt and pepper
- 2 tsp cumin
- 3 tbsp lemon juice
- 6 tbsp quinoa flour
- 1 cup green peas (can be frozen)
- 1 tsp red pepper flakes
- About 2 tablespoons grapeseed or extra vinegar olive oil

SHOPPING LIST

- Quinoa
- 1 medium Sweet Potato
- fresh Ginger
- Garlic
- Green Onions
- salt and pepper
- Cumin
- Lemon Juice
- Quinoa Flour
- Green Peas
- Red Pepper Flakes
- Grapeseed or Extra Virgin Olive Oil
- Cilantro

DIRECTIONS

Peel and cut sweet potato in half and cook in boiling water until fork-soft, about 12 minutes. Transfer to a food processor.

Add the chickpeas, ginger, garlic, green onions, salt, red pepper flakes, cumin and lemon juice to the sweet potato and process until blended. Alternative is to use a potato masher along with all ingredients

Transfer mixture to a bowl and add in quinoa and quinoa flour. Mix well and add in green peas. Feel free to taste for needed salt and pepper. Formulate burgers on a single layer sheet

In a medium skillet over medium heat, add oil until hot.

Place burgers in pan and cook until crisp and evenly, about 2 minutes then turn burgers over to cook on other side for about 2 minutes and until golden brown. Add more oil if needed.

Place the burgers in the oven and bake at 400 degrees for 10 minutes. Remove from stove and allow to sit for a few minutes. Breathe, Serve and Enjoy!

BLACK-EYED PEAS AND KALE

RECIPE

Servings 6 | Prep Time 1 hour | Total Time 2 ½ hours

INGREDIENTS

- 3 cups uncooked black-eyed peas
- 5 cups vegetable broth or 3 cups vegetable broth (Instant Pot)
- 2 cups kale, shredded
- 1 large onion, diced
- 1 tbsp ground cayenne pepper or 2 habanero peppers, minced
- 3 garlic cloves, minced
- 1 tbsp extra virgin olive oil
- ½ tsp cumin
- 1 tsp basil
- 1 bay leaf
- 1 tsp parsley
- 1 tsp thyme
- 2 tbsp arrow root
- sea salt and pepper to taste

SHOPPING LIST

- 3 cups uncooked black-eyed peas
- 5 cups vegetable broth or 3 cups vegetable broth (Instant Pot)
- 2 cups kale, shredded
- 1 large onion, diced
- 1 tbsp ground cayenne pepper or 2 habanero peppers, minced
- 3 garlic cloves, minced
- 1 tbsp extra virgin olive oil
- ½ tsp cumin
- 1 tsp basil
- 1 bay leaf
- 1 tsp parsley
- 1 tsp thyme
- 2 tbsp arrow root
- sea salt and pepper to taste

DIRECTIONS FOR STARCH MIXTURE

Dissolve the arrow root starch or cornstarch in 2 ½ tbsp water and add to pan. Stir until the sauce turns glossy, about 10 seconds.

INSTANT POT DIRECTIONS

Wash beans and put them in a large pot. Cover with water and bring to a boil. Boil for 3 to 5 minutes and turn off the heat, cover and let beans sit for 15 minutes.

After the beans have sat, rinse and drain the water, add to Instant Pot.

Stir in all additional ingredients to the Instant Pot including Potatoes, starch mixture, broth (water and bullion) and pepper. Set Instant Pot setting to Beans and timer to 30 minutes.

Breath, Serve and Enjoy!

DIRECTIONS

Wash beans and put them in a large pot. Cover with water and bring to a boil. Boil for 3 to 5 minutes and turn off the heat, cover and let beans sit for 1 hour.

After the beans have sat, drain the water and sit the beans to the side.

Add the oil to a pot and sauté onions and garlic and hot peppers for about two minutes or stir in cayenne pepper. Stir in basil, thyme, bay leaf, cumin, parsley, pepper and then add kale. Add the beans and starch mixture and cover with broth.

Bring to a boil, stir, reduce heat, cover and cook on simmer for 1 ½ hours.

Check on broth level, stirring and add more broth if needed and just enough to keep about 2 inches of broth above the beans and kale as they cook. The broth mixture should be thick and not dry.

Continue to cook until beans and potatoes are tender, adding more salt if needed. Breath, Serve and Enjoy!

WARM KALE-COLLARD SALAD

MY STORY

I'm always looking for creative ways to eat salads and what better way than to enjoy a warm salad of fresh organics. I enjoy plant based easy meals and this warm marinated salad is packed with nutrients making it completely tasty and filling! I'm all about preparing dinner for the family that fits our busy lifestyles and thankful that over the last eight years of being vegan I have educated my family about the importance to include greens as part of our daily meal.

SHOPPING LIST

- Collards Greens
- Kale
- Red Onion
- Carrots
- Garlic
- Mushrooms (any kind)
- Cherry Tomatoes
- Grapeseed Oil or Extra Virgin Olive Oil
- avocado
- Tamari Sauce
- Rice Vinegar

RECIPE

Serving 4 | Prep Time 10 mins | Total Time 15 mins

INGREDIENTS

- Two handfuls of collards, shredded
- Two handfuls of kale, shredded
- 1/2 red onion, diced
- 2 garlic cloves, minced

- 1/2 cup shredded carrots
- 1/2 cup mushrooms sliced
- Handful of cherry tomatoes, sliced
- 1 avocado, sliced
- 2 tbsp tamari
- 1 tsp grapeseed oil or extra virgin olive oil
- 2 tbsp rice vinegar
- pepper to taste

DIRECTIONS

Combine all ingredients, except pear and avocado, in a large bowl, mix well and allow to marinate for 10 minutes. In a medium heated pan, transfer ingredients from bowl into pan and cook for about 2 minutes, just enough to warm. Toss in the avocado slices and stir for 1 minute and enjoy!

STIR FRY COLLARDS – OHH GREENS!

RECIPE

Servings 4 | Prep Time 15 | Total Time 20

INGREDIENTS

- 1 bunch collard greens, cleaned and shredded
- 3 tbsp tamari sauce (gluten free)
- 2 tbsp rice vinegar (no sugar)
- 1 tsp cumin
- ½ sweet onion, minced
- 1 cube vegan bouillon (by Edward & Sons Natural Bouillon Cubes) or 1/3 cup vegetable broth
- 2 garlic cloves, minced
- few dashes of tabasco
- 2 tbsp extra virgin olive oil
- 1 tsp thyme
- Pepper to taste
- 1/3 cup water

SHOPPING LIST

- 1 bunch Collards
- Sweet Onions
- Extra virgin olive oil
- Tamari Sauce
- Vegan or Vegetarian Bouillon
- Garlic
- Cumin
- Thyme
- Rice Vinegar
- Tabasco sauce

DIRECTIONS

Wash then shred collards. In a medium bowl, mix all ingredients well, except bouillon and water and allow to cook for 10 minutes.

Over medium heat, stir in all ingredients, add bouillon cube with water. Stir-fry enough to keep the bright green color, about 3 to 5 minutes. Remove from heat and serve. Breathe and Enjoy!

OHH COLORFUL BLACK BEAN, SWEET CORN, BEETS & SPINACH SALAD!

RECIPE

Servings 6 | Prep Time 10 mins | Total Time 15 mins

INGREDIENTS

- 1 can black beans (organic) rinsed, drained
- 1 can sweet (organic) corn, rinsed, drained
- 1/2 can beets (organic) sliced and save rest to mix in a smoothie!
- 1/2 red onion, diced
- 1 1/2 cups spinach or a big handful
- 3 garlic cloves
- 1 tsp cumin
- 1/2 tsp cilantro
- 1/2 tsp oregano
- Himalayan salt or sea salt and pepper to taste
- 1/2 tsp red pepper flakes
- 2 tsp tamari
- 2 tsp rice vinegar
- 1 1/2 tbsp extra virgin oil
- 1/3 cups cashews, chopped (unsalted)

SHOPPING LIST

- Can of Organic Black Beans
- Can of Organic Corn
- Can of Organic Beets
- Red Onion
- Spinach
- Garlic
- Cumin
- Cilantro
- Oregano
- Tamari
- Rice Vinegar
- Cashews
- Extra virgin olive oil

DIRECTIONS

Mix all ingredients well and let sit for 10 minutes. Breathe, serve and enjoy!

OHH CREAMY CURRY CHICKEN SALAD!

MY STORY

A plant-based chicken salad was one of the first meals tasted when I switched to a vegan diet back in February 2009. Today, I still enjoy this dish but kicked it up a notch to add more moisture and flavor! While I use Delight Soy Nuggets, purchased in bulk directly from Whole Foods, I have also used Beyond Meat & Gardein's brands) – prepare per package and cut/dice in chucks.

SHOPPING LIST

- Soy Chicken
- Vegenaise (Follow Your Heart vegan mayo)
- Sun Dried Tomatoes
- 2 Celery stalks
- 1 Onion
- Garlic
- Curry Powder
- Parsley
- Cilantro
- Thyme
- Agave (raw)
- Red Pepper Flakes
- Paprika

RECIPE

Servings 6 | Prep Time 15 mins | Total Time 20 mins

INGREDIENTS

- 1 package Chicken from Beyond Meat, Gardein or Delight Soy Chicken Nuggets
- Fresh bunch of greens/lettuce
- 1-cup vegan mayo (Follow Your Heart Vegenaise Grape seed oil flavor)
- ½ cup sun dried tomatoes, chopped
- ¼ cup celery
- 1 tbsp. ground curry powder – or more to taste
- 1 tsp dried parsley

- 1 tsp dried thyme
- ½ onion or 1 tbsp. onion powder
- 2 garlic cloves or 1 tsp. garlic powder
- 1 tsp cilantro
- Sea Salt and pepper to taste
- 1 tsp. red pepper flakes
- 1 tsp. paprika
- 1 tbsp agave to taste

DIRECTIONS

Combine all ingredients well, sprinkle with parsley. Can eat warm or allow to chill. Serve over a bed of greens. Breathe and Enjoy!

STUFFED MARINATED COLLARD GREENS!

MY STORY

Ohh Collards! One true and tried staple in the soul food community and on restaurant menus for many years. Not only are collards delicious, but did you know collards are nutritious and low in calories and contain no cholesterol. These green leaves contain a very good amount of soluble and insoluble dietary fiber that helps control LDL cholesterol levels and offer protection against hemorrhoids, constipation as well as colon cancer diseases. Try this Ohhlicious Stuffed Marinated Collard recipe and enjoy!

SHOPPING LIST

Filling:
- Collard Greens, about 12 leaves
- Beyond Meat protein crumbles or any ground meatless crumbles
- Coconut Oil
- Garlic
- Onion
- Celery
- Carrots
- "No Chicken" Broth or Vegetable Broth
- Cayenne
- Basil
- Thyme
- Brown Rice
- Parsley Leaves
- Pepper
- For Marinate Sauce:
- Orange Juice
- Tamari Sauce
- Garlic
- Rice Vinegar

RECIPE

Servings 6 | Prep Time 15 | Total Time 45 mins

INGREDIENTS

- Ingredients for Filling:
- 1 bunch collard greens, about 12 leaves, stalks discarded
- 1 1/2 tbsp coconut oil
- 1 pack Beyond Meat protein crumbles or any ground meatless crumbles
- 2 cloves garlic, minced
- 1 large onion, chopped
- 2 stalks celery, chopped
- 2 medium carrots, chopped
- 1 cup "no chicken" broth or vegetable broth
- ¼ tsp cayenne
- 1-tsp basil
- 1-tsp thyme
- 2 cups brown rice, cooked
- ¼ cup chopped fresh parsley leaves
- pepper to taste
- Ingredients: Marinate Sauce
- 1/3 cup freshly squeezed orange juice
- 3 tbsp tamari sauce
- 1 clove garlic, minced
- 3 tbsp rice vinegar

DIRECTIONS

Marinate Sauce:

Mix all ingredients well and sit

Marinated Collards:

Cut or pull greens away from stem keeping greens in large pieces. Place collards in large bowl and pour in marinate sauce and mix well. Allow to sit for 3 to 5 minutes. Carefully transfer 12 large marinated leaves to a baking sheet lined with paper towels.

Collards Filling:

Heat coconut oil in a heavy-bottomed pan over medium –high heat. Add the meat crumbles and brown then add garlic, onion, celery, carrots, basil, thyme.

Cook for about 2 minutes with pepper to taste.

Add the no chicken broth or vegetable broth and cayenne. Stir in the cooked rice and parsley, mixing thoroughly letting the broth reduce until there is no moisture left in the pan.

Arrange a reserved collard leaf on your work surface and top with 1/3 cup rice filling.

Roll up, starting with the large end of the leaf and rolling it over the filling, tucking in the ends, like a burrito. Repeat with remaining leaves and filling and serve. Breathe and Enjoy!

OHH EATS... LIMA BEAN SOUP!

MY STORY

Love Lima Bean Soup, We Do! Lima beans has always been another "go to" dish in my home. It's flavorful and I enjoy combining both butter beans (original name) with green lima beans for an intense lima bean taste. Three reasons I enjoy lima beans is because they are low in fat; contain no cholesterol, which is why they add to the role in a heart-healthy diet; and as a vegan the fact that a serving of lima beans contains a great amount of protein is wonderful.

SHOPPING LIST

- Dry Lima Beans
- 3 Carrots
- Garlic
- Bulb Leek
- Shallot
- 2 Celery stalks
- Rosemary
- Vegetable Broth
- Extra virgin olive oil

Thanks to my Instant Pot, these raw beans were made in less than 30 minutes.

RECIPE

Servings 8 | Prep Time 15 | Total Time 3 hours 45 min (with Instant Pot – 45 mins)

INSTANT POT INGREDIENTS

- 1 pound dry lima beans
- 2 cups vegetable broth or 3 cubes vegetable bouillon (with 2 cups water)
- 3 carrots, chopped
- 2 garlic cloves, copped

- 1 leek, bulb only, chopped
- 2 tbsp minced shallots
- 2 stalks celery, chopped
- 1 tsp rosemary
- 2 tbsp extra virgin olive oil
- 4 cups water

REGULAR INGREDIENTS

- 1 pound dry lima beans
- 4 cups vegetable broth or 4 cubes vegetable bouillon (with 4 cups water)
- 3 carrots, chopped
- 2 garlic cloves, copped
- 1 leek, bulb only, chopped
- 2 tbsp minced shallots
- 2 stalks celery, chopped
- 1 tsp rosemary
- 2 tbsp extra virgin olive oil
- 4 cups water

INSTANT POT DIRECTIONS

Bring 4 cups of water to a boil. Add dry lima beans and boil for 2 to 3 minutes. Remove from heat and allow beans to sit, covered, for 5 minutes. Drain and rinse until water runs clear, discarding bean water.

In a pan on low to med heat, saute vegetables in extra virgin olive oil until onions, garlic and celery are translucent. Add lima beans and rosemary and saute for another 2 to 3 minutes.

Place all ingredients into the Instant Pot. Add the vegetable bouillon and 2 cups water or 2 cups vegetable broth. Stir and cook beans per bean selection setting timer on 30 minutes. Breath, Serve and Enjoy!

DIRECTIONS

Bring 4 cups of water to a boil. Add dry lima beans, and boil for 2 to 3 minutes. Remove from heat, and allow the beans to sit, covered, for up to 2 hours to soften. Drain and rinse until water runs clear, discarding bean water.

In a soup pot, sauté vegetables in extra virgin olive oil until onions, garlic and celery are translucent. Add lima beans and rosemary and sauté for another 2 to 3 minutes.

In the interim, add 4 cups of water and the vegetable bouillon to the pot and allow to boil, stirring (Or add 4 cups of vegetable broth and bring to a boil). Add sautéed vegetables and beans and allow soup to simmer over a low flame for 1 to 1 1/2 hours. Breathe, Serve and Enjoy!

OHH EATS PESTO PASTA

MY STORY

I absolutely love Pasta and over the years eat as little white pasta due to its, for lack of better words, "no nutritional value". My favorite versions of pasta have been rice, quinoa, soba and sprouted whole grain pastas. I am especially fond of what I drizzle, blend, mix and stir in my pasta as it relates to healthy blends…Pesto!!

SHOPPING LIST

- Pasta
- Pine Nuts
- Extra virgin olive oil
- Garlic
- Nutritional Yeast
- Hand full of Cherry Tomatoes
- Basil Leaves
- Sea Salt
- Pepper

My children too have always enjoyed white pasta and now share in the flavor of plant-based pastas with marinara, garlic & butter (plant-based), cheddar cheese (plant-based), alfredo (plant-based) and pesto. Speaking of Pesto, this Gluten Free Basil Pesto made with Quinoa Pasta is divinely flavorful, ohhlicious and kid friendly!

I am also a fond user of nutritional yeast, mainly because of its wondrous nutritional value and benefits as being an excellent source of protein, dietary fiber, vitamins and minerals. Did you know nutritional yeast is naturally fat-free and sodium-free? Its source of Vitamin B-12 is essential for vegans, plant-based eaters and can produce a healthy nervous system, proper food metabolism, and can construct and regenerate red blood cells. I use nutritional yeast as a substitute for many recipes requiring dairy, including mac & cheese, lasagna, organic popcorn and baked kale chips, which my sons enjoy!

I find pleasure in flavor and adding nutritional yeast to my pesto sauce has often received the "ohh node of approval" for it's great taste in this Gluten Free Pesto Pasta dish!

RECIPE

Servings 4 | Prep Times 20 mins | 30 mins

INGREDIENTS

- 2 cups Pasta – cook
- per package
- 1/3 pine nuts, toasted
- 2/3 cup extra virgin olive oil
- 5 cloves garlic
- hand full of cherry tomatoes
- 1/3 cup nutritional yeast
- 1 bunch fresh basil leaves
- sea salt and pepper to taste

DIRECTIONS

Place the pine nuts in a skillet over medium heat and stir constantly until lightly toasted. Mix the pine nuts, extra virgin olive oil, garlic, nutritional yeast, and basil in a food processor until smooth. Taste for yourself and season with salt and pepper. Makes enough to pour over 2 cups pasta. Less than a 30-minute meal! Breathe, Serve and Enjoy!

TWO WORDS: PINTO BEANS!

MY STORY

Did you know a half-cup of cooked pinto beans offer about 8 grams of protein, about half a gram of fat and no cholesterol, making pinto beans a good alternative to animal proteins, which are higher in unhealthy saturated fats.

As a DC Girl now living in the South, the weather can get brisk, especially lately, making it the perfect time for bean soups and stews.

SHOPPING LIST

- 1 package/12 oz Pinto Beans
- Cumin
- Chili Pepper Flakes
- Paprika
- Garlic Powder
- Onion Powder
- Oregano
- Extra virgin Olive Oil
- Onion
- Garlic
- Cilantro, chopped

RECIPE

Servings 8 | Prep Time 15 mins | Total Time 45 mins

INGREDIENTS

- 1 package/12 oz pinto beans
- 2 tbsp cumin
- 1 tsp dried chili pepper flakes
- 2 tsp paprika
- 3 tsp garlic powder
- 1 tsp onion powder
- 1 tsp oregano
- 2 tbsp extra virgin olive oil

- 1 large onion, diced
- 3 garlic cloves, chopped
- 3 tsp cilantro, chopped
- 4 to 6 cups water

INSTANT POT DIRECTIONS

Bring 4 cups of water to a boil. Add dry pinto beans and boil for 2 to 3 minutes. Remove from heat and allow beans to sit, covered, for 10 minutes. Drain and rinse until water runs clear, discarding bean water.

Place all ingredients into the Instant Pot. Add the vegetable bouillon and 2 cups water or 2 cups vegetable broth. Stir and cook beans per bean setting and increase timer to 30 minutes. Breath, Serve and Enjoy!

DIRECTIONS

Bring 4 cups of water to a boil. Add dry pinto beans and boil for 2 to 3 minutes. Remove from heat and allow the beans to sit, covered, for up to 1 hour to soften. Drain and rinse until water runs clear.

In a soup pot, add all ingredients to the beans, mixing well.

Add 4 cups of water and the vegetable bouillon to the pot and allow to boil, stirring (or add 4 cups of vegetable broth and bring to a boil). Add sautéed vegetables and beans and allow beans to simmer over a low flame for 1 to 1 1/2 hours or until beans are tender. Breathe, Serve and Enjoy!

MARINATED COLLARD GREENS

MY STORY

I love the flavor of this Marinated Collard Salad. Yum!

RECIPE

Servings 5 | Prep Time 10 mins | Total Time 25 mins

INGREDIENTS

- 2 bunches collards, shredded
- 1 cup sun dried tomatoes, sliced
- 2 garlic cloves, finely diced
- 1 lemon, juiced
- 2 1/2 tbsp tamari
- 3 tbsp extra virgin olive oil
- 2 tbsp rice vinegar
- ½ cup sweet onion, sliced
- 1 tsp oregano
- 1 tsp basil
- ½ tsp turmeric
- dash or two tabasco sauce
- 1 tsp agave
- 1 tsp flax seed (ground)
- salt and pepper to taste

SHOPPING LIST

- 2 bunches Collards
- Sun Dried Tomatoes
- Garlic cloves
- 1 Lemon
- Tamari
- Extra Virgin Olive Oil
- Rice Vinegar
- 1 Sweet Onion
- Oregano
- Basil
- Turmeric
- dash or two Tabasco Sauce
- 1 tsp Agave
- 1 tsp Flax Seed (ground)
- Salt and Pepper

DIRECTIONS

In a medium bowl, whisk all above ingredients, except collards. Set aside to marinate

Remove most stems from leaves and shred. Stems contain excellent source of vitamins.

Combine collards with marinate and with your hands, mix all ingredients well and allow to sit for 15 minutes. Breathe, Serve and Enjoy!

ARTICHOKE AND SPINACH CASSEROLE

RECIPE

Servings 6-8 | Prep Time 10 mins | Total Time 30 mins

INGREDIENTS

- 1 (12 ounce) package frozen chopped spinach - thawed, drained and squeezed dry
- 1 (8 ounce) jar marinated artichoke hearts, drained and chopped
- 1 tbsp extra virgin olive oil
- 1 (12 ounce) package light silken tofu, squeezed and drained
- 1/2 cup shredded vegan mozzarella style cheese
- 1/2 cup nutritional yeast flakes
- ½ onion
- 3 garlic cloves
- 1 tsp mustard
- 1 tbsp lemon juice
- ¼ cup water
- 1 tsp dried basil
- 1 tsp dried parsley
- ½ tsp cayenne pepper
- 1 tsp paprika
- ½ tsp sea salt

SHOPPING LIST

- 1 (12 ounce) package frozen chopped Spinach
- 1 (8 ounce) jar marinated Artichoke Hearts
- 1 (12 ounce) package light Silken Tofu
- Vegan Mozzarella Style Cheese, shredded
- Nutritional Yeast Flakes
- 1 Onion
- Extra Virgin Olive Oil
- Garlic
- Mustard
- 1 Lemon
- Basil
- Parsley
- Cayenne Pepper
- Paprika
- Sea Salt
- Black Pepper

- 1/2 tsp black pepper

DIRECTIONS

Preheat oven to 400F. Heat a medium to large skillet, adding extra virgin olive oil. Sautee onions and garlic until caramelized. Add spinach and artichoke hearts to skillet, stirring to combine. Add tofu and mash with a wooden spoon, stirring well with all ingredients in skillet. Add water, nutritional yeast flakes, mayo, vegan mozzarella cheese, including all additional ingredients. Stir together until smooth and creamy then add salt and pepper to taste. Sprinkle with remaining vegan mozzarella cheese and paprika. Bake 20 minutes. Breathe, Serve and Enjoy!

SAY YES TO BRUSSELS SPROUTS & PEAS!

RECIPE

Servings 4 | Prep Time 10 mins | Total Time 20 mins

INGREDIENTS

- 1 package organic frozen peas

- About 15 brussels sprouts or 2 cups brussels sprouts, shredded

- 1 tbsp vegan butter

- 2 garlic cloves, minced

- Sea salt and fresh cracked pepper to taste

SHOPPING LIST

- 1 package organic frozen Peas
- About 15 Brussels sprouts or 2 cups s sprouts
- Vegan butter (dairy free)
- Garlic
- Sea salt and fresh cracked pepper

DIRECTIONS

Heat medium pan with vegan butter

Add garlic until caramelized.

Add shredded Brussel sprouts and cook on medium high for 3 minutes, stirring.

Add in frozen peas and stir well.

Sauté for 3 minutes, toss lightly.

Reduce heat, cover and allow to cook on low heat for 1 minute.

Season with salt and pepper. Breathe, Serve and Enjoy!

CURRY VEGETABLES - SPICES FOR THE SOUL

RECIPE

Servings 6 | Prep Time 10 mins | Total Time 25 mins

INGREDIENTS

- 1 can Garbanzo Beans, organic (rinsed and drained)
- 3 carrot stalks, chopped
- 2 celery stalks, chopped
- 1 head of cauliflower, cut in small pieces
- 1 cup mushrooms, sliced
- ½ onion, diced
- 3 garlic cloves, minced
- 3 cups vegetable broth
- 2 tbsp curry powder
- 1 tbsp guan powder
- 1 tsp thyme
- 1 tsp basil
- ½ turmeric
- 1 tbsp fresh cilantro
- 2 tbsp arrow root
- 2 tbsp extra virgin olive oil
- 1 tsp red pepper flakes, more to taste
- pepper to taste\

SHOPPING LIST

- 1 can Garbanzo Beans, organic
- 3 carrot stalks
- 2 celery stalks
- 1 head of cauliflower
- 1 package mushrooms
- 1 onion
- Garlic cloves
- Vegetable Broth
- Curry Powder
- Garam Masala
- Thyme
- Basil
- Turmeric
- Fresh Cilantro
- Arrow Root
- Extra virgin olive oil
- Red Pepper Flakes
- Pepper to taste

DIRECTIONS

Heat medium sized skillet over high heat until hot. Reduce to medium heat and add extra virgin olive oil. Add onions and garlic until lightly colored. Stir in carrots, cauliflower, celery and mushrooms and garbanzo beans for 2 to 3 minutes or until caramelized. Add broth, curry powder, guan powder, thyme, basil, turmeric and red pepper flakes and stir well. Add arrow root mixture and continue to mix well. Bring to a simmer, tossing to combine, cover and allow to cook for 10 to 15 minutes. Remove from heat and add fresh cilantro, salt and pepper to taste. Breathe, Serve and Enjoy!

DIRECTIONS FOR STARCH MIXTURE

Dissolve the arrow root starch or cornstarch in 2 ½ tbsp water and add to pan. Stir until the sauce turns glossy, about 10 seconds.

LIMA AND COLLARDS – OHH MY!

RECIPE

Servings 6 to 8 | Prep Time 1 hour 15 mins (regular) 15 mins for (Instant Pot) | Total Time 3.5 hours (regular) 55 mins (Instant Pot)

INGREDIENTS

- 1 (1 lb) bag regular lima beans or 1 (1 lb) bag frozen lima beans
- 1 bunch Collard greens, organic – stem on and shredded
- 1 medium onion, chopped
- 2 vegan bullion (chicken flavor) or 2 vegetable bullions with 3 cups water OR 3 cups vegetable broth
- 3 garlic cloves, minced
- 1 tsp red pepper flakes
- 1 table spoon extra virgin olive oil
- 1 tsp basil
- 1 tsp thyme
- pepper to taste

SHOPPING LIST

- 1 (1 lb) bag Lima Beans or 1 (1 lb) bag frozen Lima Beans
- 1 bunch Collard Greens, organic
- 1 medium Onion
- 2 vegan Bullion (no chicken flavor) or 2 vegetable Bullions or 3 cups Vegetable Broth
- 3 Garlic cloves
- Red Pepper Flakes
- Extra Virgin Olive Oil
- Basil
- Thyme
- Pepper

INSTANT POT DIRECTIONS

Wash beans and put them in a large pot. Cover with water and bring to a boil. Boil for 3 to 5 minutes and turn off the heat, cover and let beans sit for 15 minutes.

After the beans have sat, rinse and drain the water, add to Instant Pot.

Stir in all additional ingredients to the Instant Pot including Collards, broth and pepper. Set Instant Pot setting to Beans and timer to 40 minutes.

Breath, Serve and Enjoy!

DIRECTIONS

Wash beans and put them in a large pot. Cover with water and bring to a boil. Boil for 3 to 5 minutes and turn off the heat, cover and let beans sit for 1 hour.

After the beans have sat, drain the water and sit the beans to the side.

Add the oil to a pot and sauté onions and garlic for about two minutes. Stir in red pepper flakes, basil, thyme and then add Collards together. Add the beans and cover with water and bullions OR add the vegetable broth.

Add pepper to taste

Bring to a boil, stir, reduce heat, cover and simmer for about 2 hours.

Check on water level, stirring and add more water if needed and just enough to keep about 1 inch of water above the beans as they cook.

Continue to cook until beans are tender, adding more salt if needed. Breath, Serve and Enjoy!

BLACK-EYED PEAS WITH TURNIPS

MY STORY

This was a New Year's Day staple in our home growing up. It is what I cook for my family as long as I can remember for the first day of every new year! Call it tradition, these field peas are viewed more as a seasonal delicacy and we grew up eating it combined with a slow smoked piece of meat. Nevertheless, this is food with a deep-rooted history.

SHOPPING LIST

- 1 package dry uncooked black-eyed peas
- 5 cups vegetable broth
- 4 Potatoes, organic
- 1 large onion
- Ground Cayenne Pepper or 2 Habanero Peppers
- 3 Garlic Cloves
- Extra virgin olive oil
- Cumin
- Basil
- Parsley
- Thyme
- Arrow root
- Sea Salt and Pepper

Turnips are a great source of minerals, antioxidants, and dietary fiber and ohhlicious with Black-Eyed Peas.

RECIPE

Servings 6 to 8 | Prep Time 1 hour 15 mins (regular) 15 mins (Instant Pot) | Total Time 3.5 hours (regular) 45 mins (Instant Pot)

INGREDIENTS

- 3 cups dry uncooked black-eyed peas
- 5 cups vegetable broth or 3 cups vegetable broth (Instant Pot)
- 4 Potatoes, organic, cut
- 1 large onion, diced

- 1/4 tbsp ground cayenne pepper or 2 habanero peppers, minced
- 3 garlic cloves, minced
- 1 tbsp extra virgin olive oil
- ½ tsp cumin
- 1 tsp basil
- 1 tsp parsley
- 1 tsp thyme
- 2 tbsp arrow root
- sea salt and pepper to taste

DIRECTIONS FOR STARCH MIXTURE

Dissolve the arrow root starch or cornstarch in 2 ½ tbsp water and add to pan. Stir until the sauce turns glossy, about 10 seconds.

INSTANT POT DIRECTIONS

Wash beans and put them in a large pot. Cover with water and bring to a boil. Boil for 3 to 5 minutes and turn off the heat, cover and let beans sit for 15 minutes.

After the beans have sat, rinse and drain the water, add to Instant Pot.

Stir in all additional ingredients to the Instant Pot including Potatoes, starch mixture, broth (water and bullion) and pepper. Set Instant Pot setting to Beans and timer to 30 minutes.

Breath, Serve and Enjoy!

DIRECTIONS

Wash beans and put them in a large pot. Cover with water and bring to a boil. Boil for 3 to 5 minutes and turn off the heat, cover and let beans sit for 1 hour.

After the beans have sat, drain the water and sit the beans to the side.

Add the oil to a pot and sauté onions and garlic and hot peppers for about two minutes or stir in cayenne pepper. Stir in basil, thyme, cumin, parsley, pepper and then add Potatoes together. Add the beans and starch mixture and cover with broth.

Bring to a boil, stir, reduce heat, cover and simmer for 1 ½ hours.

Check on broth level, stirring and add more broth if needed and just enough to keep about 2 inches of broth above the beans and potatoes as they cook. The broth mixture should be thick but not dry.

Continue to cook until beans and potatoes are tender, adding more salt if needed. Breath, Serve and Enjoy!

STEW VEGGIES WITH COLLARDS

RECIPE

Servings 4 | Prep Time 10 mins | Total Time 30 mins

INGREDIENTS

- 1 package extra firm tofu, drained and cut in cubes
- 1 bunch collard greens, shredded
- 2 bay leaves
- 1 tbsp thyme
- 1 tbsp rosemary
- 1/4 cup extra virgin olive oil
- 2 tbsp jalapenos
- 2 garlic cloves, minced
- 2 tbsp vegan butter (dairy free)
- 1 cup sweet onion, diced
- 1 cup mushrooms, sliced
- 1 cup green beans
- 2 tomatoes, cubed
- 1/4 cup flour
- 1 quart vegetable broth
- 1/2 cup carrot, peeled and diced
- 2 tbsp cilantro
- salt and pepper

SHOPPING LIST

- 1 package Extra Firm Tofu
- 1 bunch Collard Greens
- Bay leaves
- Thyme
- Rosemary
- Extra virgin olive oil
- 2 Jalapenos
- Garlic
- Vegan Butter (non-dairy)
- 1 Sweet Onion
- 1 package Mushrooms
- 1 package Green beans
- 2 Tomatoes
- Flour
- Quart vegetable broth
- 2 Carrots
- Cilantro
- Salt and Pepper

DIRECTIONS

Add extra virgin olive oil to a skillet on medium heat. Season tofu with salt and pepper, thyme and rosemary.

Add the tofu to heated skillet and sear well on all sides. Remove tofu, set aside and add the onions, garlic and jalapeno to skillet and cook to a golden caramelized color. Sprinkle the onions with the flour and stir to combine well. May need to add a more oil.

Return the tofu to the skillet, mushrooms, green beans, collards and carrots. Add broth, tomatoes and salt and pepper (to taste). Bring to a boil and reduce the heat to a slow simmer. Cook for 20 minutes, adding cilantro when ready to serve.

Breathe, Serve and Enjoy!

CURRY TOFU, QUINOA & VEGGIES!

RECIPE

Servings 4 | Prep Time 10 mins | Total Time 35 mins

INGREDIENTS

- 1 package extra firm tofu
- 1 cup quinoa, rinsed in a fine mesh strainer
- 2 tbsp coconut or extra virgin olive oil
- 1 small onion, diced
- 3 cloves garlic, minced
- 1 tbsp fresh grated ginger (or 1 tsp ground)
- 1 cup zucchini, sliced
- 1 cup turnips, diced
- 1 tsp parsley
- 1 tsp cilantro
- 1 tbsp curry powder
- Pinch cayenne or 1 dried red chili, diced
- 2 14-ounce cans coconut milk
- 1 cup vegetable broth
- Red pepper flakes

SHOPPING LIST

- 1 package extra firm tofu
- 1 cup quinoa, rinsed in a fine mesh strainer
- 1 tbsp coconut or extra virgin olive oil
- 1 small onion, diced
- 3 cloves garlic, minced
- 1 tbsp fresh grated ginger (or 1 tsp ground)
- 1 cup zucchini, sliced
- 1 cup turnips, diced
- 1 tsp parsley
- 1 tsp cilantro
- 1 tbsp curry powder
- Pinch cayenne or 1 dried red chili, diced
- 2 14-ounce cans coconut milk
- 1 cup vegetable broth
- Red pepper flakes

DIRECTIONS

Add Quinoa to medium saucepan over medium heat and toast for 3 minutes. Now prepare Quinoa per package and instead of water, use your favorite broth. Set aside.

In the meantime, heat a large saucepan or pot to medium heat and add 2 tbsp coconut oil. Add the onion, garlic, ginger, turnip and a pinch each salt and pepper and stir. Cook, stirring frequently, until softened.

Add curry powder, cayenne (or chili pepper), vegetable broth, coconut milk, another healthy pinch of salt and stir. Bring to a simmer then reduce heat slightly and continue cooking for 10-15 minutes.

Add the zucchini in the last 5 minutes. Taste and adjust seasonings as needed. Serve over quinoa. Breathe, Serve and Enjoy!

YEP, THE PERFECT VEGAN SHEPARD'S PIE

RECIPE

Servings 6 | Prep Time 15 mins | Total Time 45 mins

INGREDIENTS

- FILLING
- 1 medium onion, diced
- 2 cloves garlic, minced
- 2 celery stalks
- 1 tbsp cilantro
- 1 tbsp parsley
- 4 cups vegetable broth
- 2 tsp fresh thyme or 1 tsp dried thyme
- 1 10-ounce bag frozen mixed veggies: peas, carrots, green beans and mushrooms

SHOPPING LIST

- 1 medium Onion
- 2 Garlic Cloves
- 2 Celery Stalks
- Cilantro
- Parsley
- 4 cups Vegetable Broth
- Fresh Thyme or dried thyme
- 1 10-ounce bag frozen mixed veggies: peas, carrots, green beans and mushrooms
- 3 pounds Yukon Gold potatoes
- Vegan Butter
- Salt and pepper

- 3 pounds Yukon gold potatoes, thoroughly washed
- 2-4 tbsp vegan butter (non-dairy)
- Salt and pepper to taste

DIRECTIONS

Slice potatoes in half, place in a large pot and fill with water until they're just covered. Bring to a low boil on medium high heat then generously salt, cover and cook for 20-30 minutes or until tender

Once cooked, drain, add back to the pot to evaporate any remaining water, then transfer to a mixing bowl. Use a masher to mash until smooth. Add desired amount of vegan butter (2-4 tbsp) and season with salt and pepper to taste. Loosely cover and set aside.

While potatoes are cooking, preheat oven to 425 degrees and lightly grease a 2-quart baking pan.

In a large saucepan over medium heat, sauté onions and garlic in 1 tbsp extra virgin olive oil until caramelized.

Add a pinch of salt and pepper. Add broth, thyme and stir. Bring to a low boil and reduce heat to simmer.

Add frozen vegetables, stir and cover.

To thicken the mixture, add 2-3 tbsp mashed potatoes and stir. Alternatively, take out 1/2 of the mixture and whisk in 2 tbsp flour or arrow root powder. Return to the pan and whisk to thicken.

Taste and adjust seasonings as needed.

Then transfer to oven-safe baking dish and top with mashed potatoes. Smooth down with a spoon and season with pepper and a little sea salt.

Place on a baking sheet to catch overflow and bake for 10-15 minutes or until the mash potatoes are lightly browned on top. Allow to cool before serving. The longer the thicker. Breathe, Serve and Enjoy!

SPICY CHICKPEA BURGER

RECIPE

Servings 4 | Prep Time 20 mins | Total Time 25 mins

INGREDIENTS

- 1 can chickpeas, drained, rinsed and mashed
- 1/2 red onion, finely diced
- 1 small zucchini, grated
- 3 tbsp cilantro, chopped
- 3 tbsp red wine vinegar
- 1 tbsp Sriracha sauce
- 2 tbsp natural peanut butter
- 1 sweet potato, mashed
- 1 tsp ground cumin
- 1 tsp parsley
- 1/3 cup nutritional yeast flakes
- 1 tsp garlic powder
- 1/2 cup rolled oats
- 2 tbsp extra virgin olive oil
- Salt and pepper, to taste

SHOPPING LIST

- 1 can Chickpeas, organic
- 1 Red Onion
- 1 small Zucchini
- Cilantro
- Red Wine Vinegar
- Sriracha sauce
- Peanut butter
- 1 small Sweet Potato, mashed (optional)
- Ground Cumin
- Parsley
- Nutritional Yeast Flakes
- Garlic Powder
- Rolled Oats
- Extra virgin olive oil
- Salt and pepper
-
- Sandwich Maker:
- Your favorite Bread
- Vegan Mayo (Follow Your Heart – Vegenaise)
- Lettuce and Tomato

Enjoy with your favorite bread, vegan mayo, lettuce and tomato

DIRECTIONS

Drain and rinse chickpeas, place them in a bowl and mash them with a fork.

Add all the other ingredients to the bowl.

Use your hands to mix very well.

Form into 6-8 patties.

Fry these in a pan with some oil for 3 to 5 minutes on each side then pop in oven for 10 minutes at 375 degrees. Make with your favorite bread and toppings. Breathe, Serve and Enjoy!

BAKED MAC & CHEESE

MY STORY

I have been perfecting my Grandmother's Mac & Cheese for years. Cheese lovers, this vegan version is it!

RECIPE

Servings 8-10 | Prep Time 10 mins | Total Time 35 mins

INGREDIENTS

- 2 cups shredded cheddar flavor cheese by Follow Your Heart
- 1 cup shredded cheddar flavor by Daiya
- 3 tbsp. vegan butter
- 1 tsp. yellow mustard
- Pepper to taste
- 2–3 drops Tabasco sauce
- 3 tbsp flour
- 2 cups unsweetened nondairy milk
- 1 16-oz. pkg. elbow macaroni or pasta of choice, cooked
- 1 cup Cashew Cheese Sauce (see next recipe)
- Panko breadcrumbs and paprika, for garnish

SHOPPING LIST

- Vegan Cheese - Shredded cheddar flavor cheese by Follow Your Heart
- Vegan Cheese - shredded cheddar flavor by Daiya
- Vegan butter
- Yellow Mustard
- Pepper to taste
- Tabasco sauce
- Flour
- Unsweetened Nondairy Milk
- 1 16-oz. pkg. elbow macaroni or pasta of choice
- 1 cup Cashew Cheese
- Panko Breadcrumbs
- Paprika, for garnish

DIRECTIONS

Preheat the oven to 350°F.

In a large pot, melt the vegan butter over medium heat. Add the mustard, pepper, and Tabasco sauce and mix until smooth. Whisk in the flour until combined and stir in the nondairy milk.

While stirring, bring to a boil, then reduce the heat to low and continue stirring until thickened, about 1 minute. Mix in 2 cups of the vegan cheese shreds and stir again until the "cheese" has melted and the mixture has thickened further, about 2 minutes.

Add the cooked pasta and Cashew Cheese Sauce to the mac & cheese mixture and mix well. If desired, add up to ½ cup additional nondairy milk for consistency.

Pour the mac and "cheese" into an 8-inch- by-10- inch baking dish and top with the remaining vegan cheese shreds as well as a sprinkling of panko breadcrumbs and paprika.

Bake for 30 minutes or until the "cheese" is bubbling and the top is starting to brown.

Cashew Cheese Sauce

1½ cups raw cashews

½ cup nutritional yeast

Enough water to cover the cashews and nutritional yeast in the blender

1 clove garlic

Pinch sea salt

Place all the ingredients in a blender and blend until smooth and creamy.

OHHLICIOUS CHICKPEA SPINACH SALAD!

RECIPE

Servings 2 | Prep Time 8 mins | Total Time 8 mins

INGREDIENTS

- 1 can chickpeas, organic, rinsed and drained
- Large handful of spinach
- ½ lemon *or* 1 tbsp rice vinegar
- 1 tbsp agave
- 4 tbsp extra virgin olive oil
- Pinch of cumin
- Pinch of salt
- 1 tsp red pepper flakes (or ½ tsp cayenne pepper
- Small handful of dates (chopped – optional)

SHOPPING LIST

- 1 can chickpeas, organic
- Large handful of spinach
- 1 lemon *or* Rice Vinegar
- Agave
- Grape Seed Oil or Extra virgin olive oil
- Cumin
- Sea Salt and Pepper
- Red Pepper Flakes or Cayenne Pepper
- Small handful of Dates - optional

DIRECTIONS

In a large bowl, mix all ingredients well.

Breathe, Serve and Enjoy!

BOWL OF CURRY LENTIL SOUP!

RECIPE

Servings 6 | Prep Time 10 mins | Total Time 40 mins

INGREDIENTS

- 1 tbsp coconut oil (or extra virgin olive oil)
- 1 large onion, chopped
- 2 cloves garlic, minced
- 1 tbsp fresh ginger, minced
- 2 tbsp tomato paste (or ketchup)
- 2 tbsp curry powder
- 2 tbsp garam masala
- 2 tbsp jalapeno peppers, minced
- 4 cups vegetable broth
- 1 can coconut milk
- 1 can diced tomatoes
- 1.5 cups dry red lentils
- handful of shredded carrots – about 2 carrot stalks
- salt and pepper, to taste

SHOPPING LIST

- 1 tbsp coconut oil (or extra virgin olive oil)
- 1 large onion, chopped
- 2 cloves garlic, minced
- 1 tbsp fresh ginger, minced
- 2 tbsp tomato paste (or ketchup)
- 2 tbsp curry powder
- 2 tbsp garam masala
- 2 tbsp jalapeno peppers, minced
- 4 cups vegetable broth
- 1 can coconut milk
- 1 can diced tomatoes
- 1.5 cups dry red lentils
- handful of shredded carrots – about 2 carrot stalks

DIRECTIONS

In a stockpot, heat the coconut oil over medium heat and stir-fry the onion, garlic and ginger until translucent or caramelized, a couple minutes.

Add the tomato paste (or ketchup), curry powder, garam masala and jalapeno and cook for another minute.

Add the vegetable broth, coconut milk, diced tomatoes, carrots and lentils. Cover and bring to a boil, then simmer on low heat for 20-30 minutes, until the lentils are tender. Season with salt and pepper.

VEGAN BURGER

MY STORY

I wanted to create a vegan burger that didn't taste mushy. I accomplished that with this burger.

RECIPE

Servings 4 | Prep Time 15 mins | Total Time 30 mins

INGREDIENTS

- Lentils - 1 cup fully cooked, rinsed and well drained. Can also use 1 can cooked lentils (organic)

- Wild rice or brown rice or combo - 1/2 cup cooked

- Sweet potato or Japanese yam small one— baked, peeled and cut in half

- Rolled oats -1/2 cup

- TVP (vegetable textured protein) 1/2 cup - a complete protein (can get from local health food market)

- 1/4 cup mushrooms, chopped small

- 2 garlic cloves, diced

- 1 package of organic onion soup mix

- herbs: 1 tablespoon of the following: cumin, turmeric, thyme, oregano, basil

SHOPPING LIST

- Dry Lentils or 1 can also use 1 can cooked lentils (organic)
- Wild rice or brown rice or combo - 1/2 cup cooked
- 1 small Sweet Potato or Japanese Yam
- Rolled Oats
- TVP (vegetable textured protein) 1/2 cup - a complete protein (can get from local health food market)
- 1/4 cup Mushrooms
- 2 Garlic Cloves
- 1 package of organic onion soup mix
- Cumin, Turmeric, Thyme, Oregano, Basil
- Sriracha Sauce or Barbecue Sauce
- 4 Ciabatta buns or your favorite buns
- Olive Oil
- 100% Pure Canola Oil

- 1 tbsp of Sriracha sauce or barbecue sauce
- 4 Ciabatta buns or your favorite buns
- 1 tbsp olive oil or eyeball
- 2 tbsp of 100% pure canola oil or eyeball

DIRECTIONS

Heat oven at 400 degrees

DIRECTIONS:

Lightly sauté garlic and mushrooms in medium pan or cast iron pan for about two minutes then remove from heat.

In a large mixing bowl, add all wet ingredients first: sweet potato, lentils, rice and mix well. Then add dry ingredients to wet ingredients: rolled oats, onion mixture, all herbs and mix well. Add in sautéed mushrooms, garlic and sauce and continue mix using a potato masher and/or hands. Can pulse in food processor as well but not needed. Your hands are the best mixer:)

Fold and mold together the mixture making 4 juicy burgers. Mold smaller burger to add vegan cheese between each burger to make one big cheesy burger.

Heat skillet with canola oil and place in burgers, cooking about 3 to 5 minutes on one side, flipping and cooking about 3 to 5 minutes on side then placing in oven at 400 degrees for 10 minutes.

Remove from oven to add with your heated buns and toppings! I use vegan mayo, lettuce, tomatoes and avocados. Breathe, Serve & Enjoy!

COLD CHICKPEA SALAD

RECIPE

Servings 4 | Prep Time 10 mins| Total Time 20 mins

INGREDIENTS

- 1 (15 oz) can of chickpeas, rinsed and drained
- 1 red bell pepper, chopped
- 1 yellow bell pepper, chopped
- 1/2 red onion, chopped
- 1 tbsp cilantro, chopped
- ½ cup purple cabbage, shredded
- 15 grape tomatoes, halved (about 1 cup)
- 1/3 cup pitted kalamata olives
- For the dressing:
- 1 tbsp extra virgin olive oil
- 2 tbsp freshly squeezed lemon juice
- 2 cloves garlic, minced
- 1 tsp dried oregano
- salt and pepper to taste

SHOPPING LIST

- 1 (15 oz) can of Chickpeas (garbanzo), organic
- 1 Red Bell Pepper
- 1 yellow Bell Pepper
- 1 red Onion
- Cilantro
- purple Cabbage
- 15 Grape/Cherry Tomatoes
- Kalamata Olives
- For the dressing:
- Extra virgin olive oil
- 1 Lemon
- Garlic
- Dried oregano
- Salt and Pepper

DIRECTIONS

Place all salad ingredients into a large bowl and toss to combine.

In a small bowl, whisk together extra virgin olive oil, lemon juice, garlic and oregano. Pour onto salad and toss again to well combine. Add salt and pepper to taste

Can be placed in refrigerator for 1 hour to marinate or serve immediately.

.

THE MAKINGS OF A RAW – SALAD

MY STORY

I believe every dinner should start off in the raw! You get to add whatever enhancement you deem necessary. Just make sure it's clean!

RECIPE

Servings 2 | Prep Time 15 mins | Total Time 15 mins

INGREDIENTS

- 2 avocados, opened, cut in half
- 1 yellow bell peppers
- 1 red bell pepper
- 1 large tomato, sliced
- 2 carrots, shredded
- 1 bunch kale, shredded
- half bunch of cabbage, shredded
- bean sprouts, a hand full
- ½ cup cranberries
- 1/3 cup raw Papitas (Pumpkin Seeds)

INGREDIENTS - DRESSING

- 4 tbsp tamari sauce
- 4 tbsp rice vinegar
- 3 tbsp extra virgin olive oil or grape seed oil

SHOPPING LIST

- 2 Avocados
- 1 Yellow Bell Pepper
- 1 Red Bell Pepper
- 1 large Tomato
- 2 Carrots stalks
- 1 bunch Kale
- half bunch of Cabbage
- Bean Sprouts, a hand full
- ½ Cup cranberries
- 1/3 cup raw Papitas (Pumpkin Seeds)
- Tamari Sauce
- Rice Vinegar
- Extra virgin olive oil or Grape Seed Oil
- Agave
- 1 Lemon
- Pepper

- 2 tsp agave
- juice from a lemon
- pepper to taste

DIRECTIONS - DRESSING

Mix by hand the; whisk together in a bowl these ingredients together in a bowl the tamari, rice vinegar and agave. Add oil to bowl while whisking to emulsify the dressing. Toss over salad.

DIRECTIONS

Mix all ingredients – well. Breathe, Serve and Enjoy!

THE BEST SALAD EVER!

RECIPE

Servings 2 | Prep Time 15 mins | Total Time 15 mins

INGREDIENTS

- Handful of dried dates (about 1/3 cup)
- 2 cups dark leafy greens
- 1 large tomatoes, sliced
- 1 cucumber, sliced
- 1 squash, sliced
- 2 carrot stalks, shredded
- ½ red onion, sliced
- 2 avocados, sliced

SHOPPING LIST

- Handful of dried dates (about 1/3 cup)
- Dark Leafy Greens
- 1 large Tomatoes
- 1 cucumber
- 1 Ssquash
- 2 Carrots
- 1 Red Onions
- 2 Avocados

INGREDIENTS

- Sweet Ginger Vinaigrette Dressing
- 1 two-inch piece of fresh ginger, peeled.
- 3 tbsp agave
- ½ tsp salt
- ½ tsp pepper
- 4 tbsp rice vinegar
- 4 tbsp extra virgin olive oil

DIRECTIONS DRESSING

- Mince ginger in a food processor – or by hand
- Add to the food processor the agave, salt, pepper, vinegar; pulse to combine. Can also just whisk these ingredients together in a bowl.
- While food processor is running, add oil gradually (or add oil to bowl while whisking), in order to emulsify the dressing.

DIRECTIONS SALAD Mix all ingredients – well.

Breathe, Serve and Enjoy!

TRI COLOR CURRY BEANS – WHAT VEGANS EAT FOR DINNER

RECIPE

Servings 6 | Prep Time 10 mins | Total Time 30 mins

IINGREDIENTS

- 2 cans tri-color beans (black, pinto, cannellini beans), rinsed and drained, organic
- 2 cups vegetable broth
- 1/2 cup minced onion
- 3 garlic cloves, minced
- Sea salt and pepper to taste
- 1 bay leaf
- 1/2 cup diced carrots
- 1/2 cup diced celery
- 2 tbsp curry powder
- 1 tbsp garam masala
- 1 tbsp basil

SHOPPING LIST

- 2 cans tri color beans (black, pinto, Cannellini beans
- 2 cups Vegetable Broth
- 1 minced Onion
- Garlic cloves
- Sea salt and pepper to taste
- Bay Leaf
- Carrots, 2 stalks
- Celery, 2 stalks
- Curry Powder
- Garam Masala
- Basil

DIRECTIONS

In a medium sauce pan, add onions, garlic, carrots and celery and cook until tender. Add all other ingredients except for beans and bring to a boil for about 2 minutes. Add rinsed and drained beans to boil for 1 minute. Simmer beans for 20 minutes on low heat, cover.

Breathe, Serve and Enjoy!

MARINATED KALE SALAD

MY STORY

This make a welcome dish for a cookout. No disappointments

RECIPE

Servings 5 | Prep Time 15 mins| Total Time 15 mins

INGREDIENTS

- 1 small bunch of dinosaur kale leaves,
- shredded
- 2 teaspoons extra virgin olive oil
- 2 tbsp lemon juice, freshly squeezed
- 2 tbsp tamari
- 1 tbsp cumin
- 1 tsp turmeric
- 1 cup sun dried tomatoes
- 2 tbsp rice vinegar
- 1 tbsp basil
- 2 garlic cloves
- 1 tsp oregano
- 1 sweet onion, chopped
- Pinch of salt and black pepper

SHOPPING LIST

- 1 small bunch of dinosaur kale leaves
- Extra virgin olive oil
- Lemon juice, freshly squeezed
- Tamari Sauce
- Cumin
- Garlic
- Turmeric
- Sun Dried Tomatoes
- Basil
- Oregano
- Rice vinegar
- 1 sweet onion
- Pinch of salt and black pepper

DIRECTIONS

Place the shredded kale in a mixing bowl and add extra virgin olive oil, lemon juice, rice vinegar and tamari sauce. Toss with your hands, massaging the kale to tenderize and

incorporate the marinade. Add sun dried tomatoes and massage a little more to coat kale. Add garlic, onions and remaining ingredients and toss gently. Let sit for 10 minutes. Season with salt and pepper. Breathe, Serve & Enjoy!

COLORFUL BEAUTY TO MIX WITH MARINATED KALE

MY STORY

For the love of family and friends! Preparing this colorful beauty to mix with marinated kale

RECIPE

Servings 4 | Prep Time 10 mins | Total Time 10 mins

INGREDIENTS

- 1 cup sun dried tomatoes
- 1 tbsp basil
- 1 tbsp oregano
- 1 sweet onion, chopped
- 2 garlic cloves, minced

SHOPPING LIST

- Sun Dried Tomatoes
- Basil
- Oregano
- 1 Sweet Onion
- Garlic Cloves

DIRECTIONS

Mix all ingredients well and add to Marinated Kale Salad or any Salad!

CHICKEN LENTIL SOUP

MY STORY

Honor your body and nourish it with food that fuel and heal, rather than harm. Lentil Vegetable Soup and a few pieces of Chicken

RECIPE

Servings 4 | Prep Time 10 mins| Total Time 40 mins

INGREDIENTS

- 2 cups plant based chicken, chopped (Gardein, cook per packet) as an option)

- 2 tbsp coconut oil (or extra virgin olive oil)

- a few seeds of Allspice

- 1 onion, chopped

- 3 cloves garlic, minced

- 2 tbsp jalapeno peppers, minced

- ½ cup red bell peppers

- 2 tbsp cilantro

- 1 tbsp cumin

- 1 tbsp turmeric

- 4 cups vegetable broth

- 1.5 cups dry lentil

- handful of shredded carrots – about 2 carrot stalks

- salt and pepper, to taste

SHOPPING LIST

- 2 cups Plant Based Chicken, chopped (I use Gardein
- Coconut Oil (or extra virgin olive oil)
- 1 Onion
- Garlic
- Allspice Seeds
- Jalapeno Peppers
- Red Bell Peppers
- Cilantro
- Cumin
- Turmeric
- 4 cups Vegetable Broth
- 1 packet dry Lentil
- Carrots, 2 stalks
- Salt and pepper

DIRECTIONS

In a stockpot, heat the oil over medium heat and stir in the onion, garlic, red bell peppers, jalapeno peppers, carrots and celery until translucent or caramelized, a couple minutes.

Add broth, cumin, turmeric Allspice seeds and bring to a boil. Add lentils, cover and continue to boil for 2 minutes. Then simmer on low heat for 20-30 minutes, until the lentils are tender. Season with salt and pepper. Breathe, Serve and Enjoy!

YES TO SIDE SALAD

MY STORY

The perfect greens and cranberry side salad.

RECIPE

Servings 2 | Prep Time 10 mins | Total Time 10 mins

INGREDIENTS

- 2 cups dark leafy mixed greens
- ½ cup cranberries
- ½ cup mushrooms, sliced
- 1/3 cup whole cashews
- 1 tbsp grapeseed oil
- 1 tbsp rice wine vinegar
- 1 tsp lemon juice

SHOPPING LIST

- Dark Leafy Mixed Greens
- Cranberries
- Whole Cashews
- Grapeseed Oil
- Rice Wine Vinegar
- Lemon Juice
- Salt and Pepper

DIRECTIONS

Mix all ingredients together well and serve

CUCUMBER TOMATO SALAD

RECIPE

Servings 2 | Prep Time 10 mins | Total Time 10 mins

INGREDIENTS

- 1 cucumber, sliced
- ½ red onion, sliced
- 1 cup cherry tomatoes, cut in halves
- 1 tbsp dill
- 1 tsp agave
- 1 tbsp rice vinegar
- 2 tbsp grapeseed oil
- 1 tbsp oregano
- salt and pepper to taste

SHOPPING LIST

- 1 Cucumber
- 1 Red Onion
- 1 cup Cherry Tomatoes
- 1 Dill
- 1 Rice Vinegar
- 1 Agave
- 2 Grapeseed Oil
- 1 Oregano
- Salt and Pepper

DIRECTIONS

Mix all ingredients together well and serve

CURRY CAULIFLOWER, PINTO BEANS, FERMENTED TOFU AND TRI-COLOR QUINOA

RECIPE

Servings 4 | Prep Time 20 mins | Total Time 20 mins

INGREDIENTS

- 1 cup quinoa, rinsed
- 1 head cauliflower, cut in pieces
- 1 can pinto beans, organic, rinsed and drained
- 1 packet extra firm tofu, drained and lightly squeezed, diced
- ½ onion, sliced
- 2 cups vegetable broth
- 2 tbsp curry powder
- 1 tsp turmeric
- 3 garlic cloves, minced
- 1 tbsp parsley
- 1 tbsp rosemary
- 2 tbsp thyme
- salt and pepper

SHOPPING LIST

- Quinoa
- 1 head Cauliflower
- 1 can Pinto Beans, organic
- 1 packet extra firm Tofu
- 1 Onion
- 2 Vegetable Broth
- Curry Powder
- Turmeric
- Garlic
- Parsley
- Rosemary
- Thyme
- Salt and Pepper

DIRECTIONS

Add Quinoa to medium saucepan over medium heat and toast for 2 minutes. Then prepare Quinoa per package and instead of water, use your favorite broth. Set aside.

Add extra virgin olive oil to a skillet on medium heat. Season tofu with salt and pepper, 1 tbsp thyme and rosemary.

Add the tofu to heated skillet and sear well on all sides. Remove tofu, set aside and add the onions, garlic to skillet and cook to a golden caramelized color. Sprinkle the onion/garlic with the flour and stir to combine well.

Return the tofu to the skillet and add cauliflower and stir for 2 minutes. Add broth, pinto beans, thyme, curry powder, turmeric and bring to a boil. Reduce heat to a slow simmer. Cook for 20 minutes. Remove from heat and add parsley, salt and pepper to taste and serve with Quinoa. Breathe, Serve and Enjoy!

SMOKED BARBECUE TEMPEH AND BLACK BEAN SLIDERS

Servings 6 | Prep Time 18 mins | Total 30 mins

MY STORY

The more I prepare vegan food, the more I only want to go to a restaurant for the vino, conversation and ambiance. Try these easy yet ohhlicious smoked sliders and let me know what you think!

INGREDIENTS

- 3 tbsp grapeseed oil or extra virgin olive oil
- 1 tbsp ground flax seeds
- 3 tbsp water
- 1-8oz package tempeh, crumbled
- 1 tsp smoked paprika
- 1 packet burger seasoning mix
- ¼ tsp black pepper
- 1 cup black beans, organic, rinsed and drained
- ½ cup onions, minced
- 3 garlic cloves, minced
- 3 tablespoons nutritional yeast flakes

SHOPPING LIST

- Grape Seed or Extra Virgin Olive Oil
- Ground Flax Seeds
- 1-8oz package Tempeh
- Smoked Paprika
- 1 packet Burger Seasoning Mix
- Black Pepper
- 1 can Black Beans, organic
- 1 Onions
- Garlic
- Nutritional Yeast Flakes
- Tamari
- Liquid Smoke
- Your favorite bbq sauce
- Rice Vinegar
- Cilantro
- Oatmeal, quick-cooking
- Vegan Mayo (Follow Your Heart – Vegenaise)
- 1 Cucumber
- Lettuce
- 1 large Tomato

- 2 tbsp tamari
- 2 tsp liquid smoke
- 1/2 cup of your favorite bbq sauce
- 1/3 cup rice vinegar
- 1 tbsp cilantro
- 1/4 cup oatmeal, quick-cooking
- ½ cup vegan mayo (Follow Your Heart – Vegenaise)
- 1 cucumber, thinly sliced
- 6 lettuce leaves
- 1 large tomato, sliced for six pieces
- 6 slider buns

DIRECTIONS

Preheat oven to 375F.

Combine ground flax seeds and or water in a small bowl. Set aside

Crumble tempeh in a large bowl. Add Paprika, burger seasoning, black pepper, black beans, onions, garlic, nutritional yeast flakes, tamari, liquid smoke, bbq sauce, rice vinegar, cilantro and oatmeal. Mix and mash well until mushy. Can also use a food processor.

Divide the mixture into 6 burgers, about an inch thick

Heat pan on medium high with oil and place burgers in pan. Brown on each side for 2 minutes then transfer to oven and allow to bake for 10 to 12 minutes.

Serve on the slider buns with vegan mayo, cucumbers, lettuce and tomatoes. Breathe, Serve and Enjoy!

ROASTED CHICKPEAS

RECIPE

Servings 6 | Prep Time 5 mins | Total Time 20 mins

INGREDIENTS

- 2 15-ounce cans chickpeas,
- Organic, rinse and drain
- 2 tbsp extra virgin olive oil
- 1 tsp sea salt
- Optional: 1/2 tsp of these to combine: chili powder, rosemary and thyme

SHOPPING LIST

- 2 15-ounce cans chickpeas, organic
  Extra virgin olive oil
  Salt
- Optional: chili powder, rosemary and thyme

DIRECTIONS

Heat the oven to 400°F

Pat dry the chickpeas with a paper towels to look matte and feel dry to the touch.

Toss the chickpeas with extra virgin olive oil and salt: Spread the chickpeas out in an even layer on the baking sheet. Drizzle with extra virgin olive oil and sprinkle with salt. Use your hands to stir to coat chickpeas then roast for 15 minutes

Stir chickpeas once. Remove from oven when chickpeas are golden dry and crispy on the outside and soft in the middle.

Optional - Sprinkle spices over the chickpeas and stir to evenly coat. Breathe, Serve and Enjoy!

MEGA GREEN SALAD

RECIPE

Servings 4 | Prep Time 10 mins | Total Time 15 mins

INGREDIENTS

- 1 bunch spinach, chopped
- 2 avocados, sliced
- 1 cup peas
- 2 cups cabbage, shredded
- ½ red onion, sliced
- 1 cup cherry tomatoes, sliced
- 1 cup shredded carrots
- 1 tbsp ground flax seeds
- 3 tbsp rice vinegar
- lemon juice from 1 lemon
- 2 tbsp extra virgin olive oil
- 2 tbsp nutritional yeast flakes
- salt and pepper to taste

SHOPPING LIST

- 1 bunch Spinach
- 2 Avocados
- Peas (can be frozen)
- 2 cups Cabbage
- 1 Red Onion
- 1 cup Cherry Tomatoes
- 1 cup shredded Carrots
- Flax Seeds
- Rice Vinegar
- 1 Lemon
- Extra Virgin Olive Oil
- Nutritional Yeast Flakes
- Salt and Pepper

DIRECTIONS

In a medium sized bowl mix all ingredients very well, including oil, nutritional yeast flakes, rice vinegar and lemon juice. Breathe, Serve and Enjoy!

RED COCONUT CURRY WITH TOFU & VEGGIES

RECIPE

Servings 4 | Prep Time 10 mins | Total Time 30 mins

INGREDIENTS

- 1 packet extra firm tofu, cubed
- 1 cup sun dried tomatoes
- 1 bay leaf
- ½ tsp all spice
- 2 tbsp red curry paste
- 1 can coconut milk
- ½ cup vegetable broth
- 3 tbsp curry powder
- 2 tbsp garam masala
- 2 – 3 dashes of Tabasco sauce
- 1 tbsp thyme
- 1 tbsp basil
- 1 tbsp onion powder
- 1 tbsp garlic powder
- 2 tbsp flour or arrow root
- salt and pepper to taste

SHOPPING LIST

- 1 packet Extra Firm Tofu, cubed
- Sun Dried Tomatoes
- Bay Leaf
- All Spice
- Red Curry Paste
- 1 can Coconut Milk
- 1 quart Vegetable Broth
- Curry Powder
- Garam Masala
- Tabasco sauce
- Thyme
- Basil
- Onion Powder
- Garlic Powder
- Flour or Arrow Root
- Salt and Pepper to taste

DIRECTIONS

In a medium pot, add coconut milk, broth, sundried tomatoes and all other ingredients, except tofu, flour, salt and pepper. Bring to a boil and whisk in flour and boil for an additional minute. Reduce heat to a slow simmer and add tofu. Cook for 20 minutes, adding salt and pepper to taste.

Breathe, Serve and Enjoy!

EGGPLANT & VEGETABLES

MY STORY

Short on cooking time but have mushrooms and eggplant handy? Why not slice them and prepare a quick mushroom and eggplant stir fry. Literally takes 15 minutes to prepare this ohhlicious healthy meal.

RECIPE

Servings 4 | Prep Time 10 mins | Total Time 20 mins

INGREDIENTS

- 2 Extra virgin olive oil
- 1/3 cup vegetable broth
- 2 tbsp liquid smoke
- 2 tbsp nutritional yeast flakes
- 1 tbsp parsley
- 1 eggplant, medium size, sliced
- 2 garlic cloves, mined
- 2 tsp jalapeno peppers
- 1 cup Portobello mushroom, sliced
- ½ cup green peas
- ¼ cup onion, diced

SHOPPING LIST

- 2 Extra Virgin Olive Oil
- Vegetable Broth
- Liquid Smoke
- Nutritional Yeast Flakes
- parsley
- 1 Eggplant, medium size
- Garlic Cloves
- 1 medium Jalapeno Pepper
- Portobello mushroom
- Green Peas
- 1 Onion

DIRECTIONS

In a medium pan, sauté onion, garlic, jalapeno peppers until tender. With medium heat, add in liquid smoke, nutritional yeast flakes and broth and cook for 2 minutes. Add mushrooms and eggplant and cook for 5 minutes. Then reduce heat to low and add in the rest of ingredients, stir lightly for about 2 minutes. Breathe, Serve and Enjoy!

BLACK-EYED PEAS

MY STORY

A beauty bowl of Black-Eyed Peas is part of the legume family and one of my favorites to eat. They are a primary source of plant protein. My family loves them too! This little bowl of ohhliciousness helps with maintaining healthy muscles, bones and cartilage. They also contain vital nutrients such as vitamins B, E, iron and potassium.

RECIPE

Servings 6-8 | Prep Time 1 hour 15 mins | Total Time 2 hour 15 mins

SHOPPING LIST

- Vegan butter
- 1 Onion
- Garlic
- 1 cup cut Green Beans, organic
- 2 stalks Celery
- 1 packet Black-Eyed Peas
- 1 Quart Vegan Broth or Vegetable Broth
- Liquid Smoke
- Cumin powder
- Parsley
- Oregano
- Salt and Pepper
- Red Pepper Flakes
- Cayenne Pepper
- Rice Vinegar
- White, Brown or Quinoa for serving

INGREDIENTS

- 4 tbsp vegan butter
- 1 onion, diced
- 4 garlic cloves, minced
- 1 cup cut green beans (can use organic frozen)
- 2 stalks celery, diced
- 4 cups black-eyed peas (see soaking directions below)

- 5 cups vegan broth or vegetable broth
- 2 tbsp liquid smoke
- 1 tsp cumin powder
- 2 tsp parsley
- 1 tbsp oregano
- salt and pepper to taste
- 2 tsp red pepper flakes
- 1 tsp cayenne pepper to taste
- 2 tbsp rice vinegar
- white, brown or quinoa for serving

DIRECTIONS FOR QUICK SOAKING BEANS

Wash beans and put them in a large pot. Cover with water and bring to a boil. Boil for 3 to 5 minutes and turn off the heat, cover and let beans sit for 1 hour. After the beans have sat, drain the water and sit the beans to the side.

DIRECTION

Heat butter in a large pot over medium-high heat. Add onion, garlic and celery and stir. Cook for 2 to 3 minutes. Stir in soaked beans, then add broth, salt & pepper, red pepper flakes, oregano, liquid smoke, cumin and cayenne to taste. Bring to a boil, then reduce heat and cover the pot for 30 minutes.

After 30 minutes, check the liquid level; if it's too soupy, cook with the lid off for another 15 minutes or so. If it's too thick, splash in a little more broth.

Stir in green beans and rice vinegar, then taste for seasonings. Add more spice if needed.

Serve over white, brown rice or quinoa. Breathe, Server and Enjoy!

VEGAN SAUCE FOR LASAGNA

RECIPE

Servings 6-8 | Prep Time 10 mins | Total Time 20 mins

INGREDIENTS

- 2 cups spinach, chopped
- 1 packet meatless crumbles, (Gardein, gluten free)
- 1 medium sweet red pepper, julienned
- 8 ounces fresh mushrooms, sliced
- 2 medium carrots, sliced very thin (or shredded)
- 32 oz tomato sauce, organic
- 1 8 oz tomato paste, organic
- 1 teaspoon dried oregano
- 2 teaspoons dried basil
- 1 teaspoon salt
- 2 tbsp lemon juice
- 2 garlic cloves, minced
- 1 small onion, minced
- 2 tbsp rosemary
- 1 ½ cup nutritional yeast flakes
- 1/4cup extra virgin olive oil

SHOPPING LIST

- 2 cups spinach, chopped
- 1 packet meatless crumbles, (Gardein, gluten free)
- 1 medium sweet red pepper,
- 8 ounces fresh mushrooms,
- 2 medium carrots
- 32 oz tomato sauce, organic
- 1 8 oz tomato paste, organic
- Dried Oregano
- Dried Basil
- Salt and Pepper
- Lemon Juice
- Garlic
- 1 Onion
- Rosemary
- Nutritional Yeast Flakes
- Extra virgin olive oil

- ½ cup water

DIRECTIONS

In a large saucepan, sauté onion, garlic, red pepper, mushrooms, zucchini, carrots in the oil until tender.

Stir in the meatless crumbles and cook until brown, scraping skillet to mix well.

Stir in the tomato sauce, tomato paste and water and add in all other ingredients.

Bring to boil, then cover, reduce heat and simmer for 25 minutes, stirring occasionally. If sauce is too thick, add more water. Breathe, Serve and Enjoy!

LIGHTLY STEAMED SUPER GREENS

RECIPIE

Servings 2 | Prep Time 10 mins | Total Time 12 mins

INGREDIENTS

2 cups spinach

1 cup carrots, shredded

1 cup strawberries, sliced

½ cup nutritional yeast flakes

1 tbsp red pepper flakes

2 tbsp rice vinegar

1 tbsp agave

2 tbsp water

1 tbsp basil

SHOPPING LIST

- 2 cups spinach
- 1 cup carrots, shredded
- 1 cup strawberries, sliced
- ½ cup nutritional yeast flakes
- 1 tbsp red pepper flakes
- 2 tbsp rice vinegar
- 1 tbsp agave
- 2 tbsp water
- 1 tbsp basil

DIRECTIONS

Mix all ingredients in a bowl then transfer to a medium heat pan. Allow to sauté until spinach is wilted. Remove from heat. Breathe, Serve and Enjoy!

GLASS FULL OF COLLARDS & BRUSSELS SPROUTS

RECIPE

Servings 4 | Prep Time 10 mins| Total Time 25 mins

INGREDIENTS

- 2 cups brussels sprouts, sliced
- 1 bunch or 2 cups collard greens, shredded, stem on
- 2 tsp vegan butter
- 2 tbsp extra virgin olive oil or grapeseed oil
- 1 vegan bullion with 1 cup water -chicken flavor or 1 cup vegetarian broth)
- ½ cup onion, sliced
- 2 tbsp rice vinegar
- 2 tbsp nutritional yeast flakes
- 1 tsp garlic powder
- 1 tsp thyme
  1 tsp red pepper flakes
- salt and pepper to taste

SHOPPING LIST

- 2 cups Brussels Sprouts
- 1 bunch or 2 cups Collards
- Vegan Butter
- Extra virgin olive oil or Grapeseed Oil
- Vegan Bullion -chicken flavor or Vegetarian Broth)
- Onion
- Nutritional Yeast Flakes
- Rice Vinegar
- Garlic Powder
- Thyme
  Red Pepper Flakes
- Salt and Pepper

DIRECTIONS

In a medium sauce pan, sauté onion with oil until tender. Stir in butter, rice vinegar, garlic powder, thyme and add Brussel sprouts and collards until veggies are wilted. Stir in bullion and water or broth along with red pepper flakes, nutritional yeast flakes and bring to a boil. Immediately reduce heat to a simmer, cover and allow to cook for broth as dissolved, about 10 minutes. Breathe, Serve and Enjoy!

ROASTED VEGETABLES & CHICKPEAS

MY STORY

Perfect dinner when there is little time to cook. What about trying these roasted vegetables with marinated chickpeas. Really a 30-minute meal including prep time!

RECIPE

Servings 4 | Prep Time 10 mins | Total Time 20 mins

INGREDIENTS

- 2 tbsp extra virgin olive oil or grape seed oil
- 3 carrots, cleaned and cut in half
- 1 large sweet potatoes, thinly sliced
- 1 cup green beans, ends cut
- ½ cup whole garlic cloves, peeled
- 1 can organic garbanzo beans rinsed, drained
- 2 tbsp grapeseed or extra virgin olive oil
- 2 tbsp basil
- 1 tbsp cayenne pepper
- 1 tsp of cumin
- 2 tbsp thyme
- salt and pepper to taste
- five small bowls

SHOPPING LIST

- 2 tbsp extra virgin olive oil or grape seed oil
- 3 carrots, cleaned and cut in half
- 1 large sweet potatoes, thinly sliced
- 1 cup green beans, ends cut
- ½ cup whole garlic cloves, peeled
- 1 can organic garbanzo beans rinsed, drained
- 2 tbsp grapeseed or extra virgin olive oil
- 2 tbsp basil
- 1 tbsp cayenne pepper
- 1 tsp of cumin
- 2 tbsp thyme
- salt and pepper to taste
- **five small bowls**

DIRECTIONS

Oven to Roasted at 400 degree or Bake at 425 degree

Spice Mix: In a small bowl, combine basil, cumin, cayenne pepper, thyme, salt and pepper and sit aside

Place beans in a bowl and mix with rice vinegar and tamari sauce and a little of the Spice Mix

Place each vegetable into a bowl and mix each vegetable with 1 tbsp spice mix and drizzle with oil.

On a large roasting pan or oven tray, place vegetables and marinated beans in a sectional space. Drizzle with additional oil, if needed. Also feel free to combine all ingredients in one bowl.

Breathe, Serve and Enjoy!

CHICKPEA & AVOCADO SANDWICH

RECIPE

Servings 4 | Prep Time 10 mins| Total Time 10 mins

INGREDIENTS

- 1 can garbanzo beans, rinsed and drained
- 1 avocado
- 1 tbsp cilantro
- 1 tsp garlic powder
- 2 tbsp green onion, chopped
- 2 tbsp parsley
- juice from 1 lime juice
- 1/2 tsp cumin
- salt and pepper to taste
- Sandwich toppings:
- fresh spinach or dark leafy lettuce of choice
- sprouts
- tomatoes, sliced
- sandwich bread of choice

SHOPPING LIST

- 1 can Garbanzo beans, organic
- 1 Avocado
- Cilantro
- Garlic Powder
- Green Onion
- Parsley
- 1 Lime
- Cumin
- Salt and Pepper

- Sandwich toppings:
- fresh spinach or dark leafy lettuce of choice
- sprouts
- tomatoes
- sandwich bread of choice

DIRECTIONS

In a medium bowl, use a big fork or potato masher to smash the chickpeas and avocado together. Add in cilantro, green onion, parsley, garlic powder, cumin and lime juice. Season with salt and pepper, to taste.

Spread salad on bread and top with your favorite sandwich toppings.

HEARTY MISO SOUP

RECIPE

Servings 6 | Prep Time 10 mins | Total Time 20 mins

INGREDIENTS

- 8 cups kombu (dashi water/Japanese broth)
- 1 packet soft tofu, drained and cut into small cubes
- 4 tbsp miso paste (white fermented-soybean paste)
- ½ cup dried seaweed (for miso soup) soaked in water
- 2 tbsp chopped green onion
- Kombu, 12 inches
- 2 tbsp instant kombu

SHOPPING LIST

- 1 packet soft Tofu
- White Miso Paste
- ½ cup Dried Seaweed
- Green Onions
- 1 Kombu about 12 inches or
- Instant/powered Kombu

Directions – Dashi WATER with kombu

Dashi is a Japanese stock and kombu is kelp, making this stock vegan. Place the kombu into the 8 cups of filtered water in a closed container and soak overnight in the fridge OR you can soak it for no less than 30 minutes at room temperature, since the kombu needs to produce all the umami on its own. Another alternative is to use kombu power, whisk to dissolve about 2 tbsp to 8 cups of filtered water and continue with directions.

Bring the dashi water to a simmer (not a full boil) and then take out the kombu, producing a light color flavored dashi. The soaked kombu can be cooked longer until soft and used in stewed dishes and soups.

DIRECTIONS - MISO SOUP

Bring the dashi to a boil then turn heat to medium-low and add the tofu. Drain the seaweed and add the seaweed to the pot. Simmer for 2 minutes.

In the interim and in a bowl, add miso paste and ½ cup of the hot dashi water and whisk to mix well melting the miso paste to become a smooth mixture.

Turn the heat off, add the miso paste to the pot and stir well. Taste the soup for flavor. If needed, whisk in another tablespoon or two of miso paste. Top with green onions. Breathe, Serve and Enjoy!

Soak and prepare Seaweed

Combine seaweed with warm water to cover by 1 inch and let stand 15 minutes, drain.

THE MAKING OF KALE CHIPS

MY STORY

Kale chips on its way into the oven and makes a great snack

RECIPE

Servings 4 | Prep Time 5 mins | Total Time 15 mins

INGREDIENTS

- 1 bunch kale, remove leaves from stems
- 1 tsp sea salt
- ¼ cup nutritional yeast flakes
- 1/4 cup grapeseed or extra vinegar olive oil

SHOPPING LIST

- 1 bunch Kale
- Sea Salt
- Nutritional Yeast Flakes
- Grapeseed or Extra Vinegar Olive Oil

DIRECTIONS

Heat oven to 400 and bake kale chips for 15 minutes

STEW VEGGIES & TOFU WITH QUINOA

RECIPE

Servings 4 | Prep Time 10 mins | Total Time 30 mins

INGREDIENTS

- 1 package extra firm tofu, drained, cut in cubes
- 1 cup tri-color quinoa or any color
- 1 cup Brussels sprouts, cut in halves
- 1 bay leaves
- 1 tbsp thyme
- 1 tbsp rosemary
- 3 tbsp extra virgin olive oil
- 3 garlic cloves, minced
- 1 cup sweet onion, diced
- 1 cup mushrooms, sliced
- 1/4 cup flour
- 1 quart vegetable broth
- 1/2 cup carrot, peeled and chopped
- 2 tbsp cilantro
- 2 tsp red pepper flakes
- salt and pepper

SHOPPING LIST

- 1 package Extra Firm Tofu
- 1 bunch Brussel Sprouts
- Tri Color Quinoa or any color
- 2 Bay Leaves
- Thyme
- Rosemary
- Extra virgin olive oil
- Garlic Cloves
- Sweet Onion
- Mushrooms- 1 Cup
- Flour
- 1 Quart Vegetable Broth
- Carrot – 2 stalks
- Cilantro
- Red Pepper Flakes
- Salt and Pepper

DIRECTIONS

Add Quinoa to medium saucepan over medium heat and toast for 3 minutes. Now prepare Quinoa per package and instead of water, use your favorite broth. Set aside.

Add extra virgin olive oil to a skillet on medium heat. Season tofu with salt and pepper, thyme and rosemary.

Add the tofu to heated skillet and sear well on all sides. Remove tofu, set aside and add the onions, garlic to skillet and cook to a caramelized color. Sprinkle the onions and garlic with the flour and stir to combine well, add more oil if needed.

Stir in the tofu, mushrooms, Brussel sprouts and carrots. Add broth, bay leaves, red pepper flakes and salt and pepper (to taste). Bring to a boil and reduce the heat to a slow simmer. Cook for 20 minutes, adding cilantro when ready to serve.

Breathe, Serve and Enjoy!

VEGAN CORNBREAD

**A Traditional Soul's Favorite and Part of my
Grandmother Gussie's Sunday Best.
Individual Recipes are throughout this book.**

MY STORY

Vegans love cornbread too! Skillet cornbread is a southern favorite. Try this ohhliciously guilt free, dairy-free and egg-free version of <u>vegan</u> skillet cornbread.

RECIPE

Servings 6-8 | Prep Time 10 mins | Total Time 35 mins

INGREDIENTS

- 1 1/2 cups soy milk
- 2 tsp lemon juice
- 1 2/3 cup flour
- 1 cup cornmeal
- 4 tsp baking powder
- 3/4 tsp salt
- 1 jalapeno pepper, diced (or to taste)
- 1 cup corn
- 1/2 cup vegetable oil
- 1/2 cup maple syrup

SHOPPING LIST

- 1 1/2 cups soy milk
- 2 tsp lemon juice
- 1 2/3 cup flour
- 1 cup cornmeal
- 4 tsp baking powder
- 3/4 tsp salt
- 1 jalapeno pepper, diced (or to taste)
- 1 cup corn
- 1/2 cup vegetable oil
- 1/2 cup maple syrup

DIRECTIONS

Pre-heat oven to 375 degrees. Lightly grease a 10-inch skillet. Place in the over to heat it up.

In a small bowl, stir together the soy milk and lemon juice.

In a separate large bowl, combine the flour, cornmeal, baking powder, salt and diced jalapeno peppers.

In a food processor or blender, puree the corn, vegetable oil and maple syrup until smooth and well combined. Add the soymilk and lemon juice, then slowly add to the flour mixture, stirring just until combined.

Pour the batter into the greased skillet, and bake for 25 minutes, or until golden brown. Enjoy your vegan skillet cornbread! Breathe, Serve and Enjoy!

VEGAN STEAK & CHEESE

RECIPE

Servings 2 | Prep Time 10 mins | Total Time 10 mins

INGREDIENTS

- vegan beef tips (Gardein) or use Seitan strips (Westsoy or any organic brand)
- vegan mozzarella shredded cheese (Daiya or Follow Your Heart)
- 2 tbsp coconut oil
- 2 tbsp vegan Worcestershire
- 1 sweet onion, sliced
- 1 medium jalapeno peppers
- 3 garlic cloves, minced
- 1 green bell pepper (can also use red or yellow bell peppers), sliced
- vegan mayo (Vegenaise by Follow Your Heart)
- 2 ciabatta buns or your choice of baguette or sub roll

SHOPPING LIST

- vegan Beef Tips (Gardein) or use Seitan strips (Westsoy or any organic brand)
- vegan Mozzarella shredded cheese (Daiya or Follow Your Heart)
- Coconut Oil
- vegan Worcestershire
- 1 medium jalapeno pepper
- 1 sweet Onion
- Garlic cloves
- Green Pepper (can also use red or yellow bell peppers)
- 2 Ciabatta buns or your choice of Baguette or Sub Rolls

DIRECTIONS

Turn oven to 450 degrees then place buns on middle rack until buns are toasted. Remove

In a skillet on medium-high heat coconut oil heat, add in onions, garlic, jalapeno and bell peppers and cook for 1 minute. Stir in beef tips or seitan and add in Worcestershire. Stir and cook until brown.

Stir in half of the bag of vegan cheese or more until the cheese melts!

Spread buns with vegan mayo and add the steak and cheese mixture. Breathe, Serve and Enjoy!

MARINATED GARLIC KALE

MY STORY

An alternative to cooking out all those good nutrients? Ohhlicious, beautiful and sexy for you. Does the body good!

RECIPE

Servings 4 | Prep Time 5 mins | Total Time 15 mins

INGREDIENTS

- 1 bunch kale, shredded
- 4 garlic cloves, minced
- 2 tbsp rice vinegar
- 2 tbsp coconut oil or grapeseed oil
- 3 tbsp tamari sauce
- 2 tbsp lime juice, fresh squeezed
- 3 tbsp tahini
- ¼ cup water
- 1 tbsp extra virgin olive oil
- ½ tsp minced ginger root
- 1 tbsp tamari
- 1 tsp organic coconut sugar
- salt and pepper to taste
- 1 tsp roasted white sesame seeds

SHOPPING LIST

- 1 bunch Kale
- Garlic
- Rice Vinegar
- Coconut oil or Grapeseed oil
- Tamari Sauce
- Lime Juice
- Tahini
- Extra Virgin Olive Oil
- Minced Ginger Root
- Organic Coconut Sugar
- Salt and Pepper
- Roasted White Sesame Seeds

DIRECTIONS - GINGER LIME TAHINI SAUCE

- 2 tbsp lime juice, fresh squeezed
- 3 tbsp tahini

- ¼ cup water
- 1 tbsp extra virgin olive oil
- ½ tsp minced ginger root
- 1 tbsp tamari
- 1 tsp organic coconut sugar
- salt and pepper to taste

In a mixing bowl, combine and whisk all ingredient together and set aside for salad

Salad: Combine shredded kale, garlic, rice vinegar, oil and tamari sauce using hands to massage. Drizzle with ginger lime tahini dressing. Breathe, Serve and Enjoy!

AVOCADO & SPICY BLACK BEAN SOUP

RECIPE

Servings 4 | Prep Time 5 mins | Total Time 17 mins

INGREDIENTS

- 2 cans black beans, organic, drained and rinsed
- 2 medium jalapenos, diced
- 1 vegan (bullion with 2 cups water) or vegetable broth (2 cups)
- 1 tsp garlic powder
- 1 tsp onion powder
- 1 tsp thyme
- 1/2 tsp chili powder
- ½ tsp cumin
- ½ tsp cayenne
- pepper and salt to taste
- ¼ cup nutritional yeast flakes
- a few dashes tabasco sauce
- 1 tbsp cilantro

SHOPPING LIST

- 2 cans black beans, organic
- 2 medium jalapenos
- 1 vegan (bullion with 2 cups water) or vegetable broth (2 cups)
- Garlic Powder
- Onion Powder
- Thyme
- Chili Powder
- Cumin
- Cayenne
- pepper and salt
- Nutritional Yeast Flakes
- Tabasco Sauce
- Cilantro

DIRECTIONS

In a saucepan, combine and bring to a boil the beans, jalapenos, vegan or vegetable broth. Add in garlic, nutritional yeast fakes, powder, onion powder, thyme, chili powder, cumin, cayenne, pepper, and tabasco sauce.

Reduce heat to a simmer and add cilantro. Continue cooking for 12 minutes. Breathe, Serve and Enjoy!

OHH KALE YEAH!

MY STORY

This marinated kale slaw is divine and with the benefits of mixing kale and with purple cabbage, carrots, red onions, avocados makes this dish even more Ohhlicious.

RECIPE

Servings 4 | Prep Time 10 mins | Total Time 15 mins

INGREDIENTS

- 1 bunch kale, shredded
- 1 cup purple cabbage, shredded
- ½ cup asparagus, chopped
- 2 carrots, shredded
- 1 small red onions, diced
- 2 avocados, chopped
- 3 tbsp tahini sauce
- 1 large orange, zest and juice combined
- 3 tbsp coconut oil, melted or grapeseed oil
- 1 tsp garlic powder
- ½ tsp coriander
- ¼ tsp ground cinnamon
- 1 tbsp cilantro, chopped

SHOPPING LIST

- 1 bunch Kale
- Purple Cabbage
- ½ cup Asparagus
- 2 Carrots
- 1 small Red Onions
- 2 Avocados
- Tahini Sauce
- 1 large Orange
- Coconut Oil or Grapeseed oil
- Garlic Powder
- Coriander
- Ground Cinnamon
- Cilantro

DIRECTIONS -CITRUS ORANGE TAHINI SAUCE

- 3 tbsp tahini sauce
- 1 large orange, zest and juice combined
- 3 tbsp coconut oil, melted or grapeseed oil
- 1 tsp garlic powder
- ½ tsp coriander
- ¼ tsp ground cinnamon
- 1 tbsp cilantro, chopped

DIRECTIONS

In a small bowl, whisk all the above ingredients together, except cilantro. Then stir in cilantro.

Allow the dressing to sit to room temperature for oil to liquefy. Breathe, Serve and Enjoy!

GRILLED CHEESE & SPINACH – WHY NOT!

RECIPE

Servings 4 | Prep Time 10 mins | Total Time 20 mins

INGREDIENTS

- Fresh spinach,
- 2 bunches, leaf
- 1 packet vegan Havarti cheese (Daiya) or any vegan cheese of choice
- 2 tbsp vegan butter
- sliced bread of choice (I used sprouted grain Ezekiel bread)
- pepper
- ½ tsp garlic powder
- ½ tsp red pepper flakes

SHOPPING LIST

- Fresh Spinach, 2 bunches
- Vegan Havarti Cheese (Daiya) or any Vegan Cheese of choice
- Vegan Butter
- Bread of choice (Sprouted Grain Ezekiel bread)

DIRECTIONS

In a large skillet on medium heat, add in 1 tablespoon water and mix with pepper, garlic powder, red pepper flakes and spinach until wilted. Remove spinach from pan.

On a large tray, place one slice on the Havarti cheese on four slices of bread followed by a scoop of spinach. Place the other Havarti cheese slice on top of the spinach and top with the other slice of bread.

Add 1 teaspoon of vegan butter to the pan. Add the sandwiches to the pan and grill on both sides until golden brown and the cheese has melted, about 2-4 minutes on each side. Add the additional vegan butter to the pan prior to turning sandwich. Breathe, Serve and Enjoy!

MARINATED COLLARDS & CHICKPEAS

MY STORY

Makes a great anytime meal or snack! So good. So good for you. So good for your body!

RECIPE

Servings 4 | Prep Time 8 mins | Total Time 15 mins

INGREDIENTS

- 2 cups collard greens
- 1 can chickpeas, organic, rinsed and drained
- ½ cup mushrooms, sliced
- ½ cup carrots, shredded
- 1 small onion, shredded
- ½ cup cherry tomatoes, sliced
- 2 tbsp rice vinegar
- 2 tbsp grapeseed oil or extra virgin olive oil
- 2 tbsp tamari
- 1 lemon squeezed
- ½ cup raw unsalted cashews, ground
- 1 pear of choice, sliced
- 1 tbsp nutritional yeast flakes

SHOPPING LIST

- Collard Greens
- 1 can Chickpeas, organic
- Mushrooms
- Carrots, about two stalks
- 1 small Onion
- Rice Vinegar
- Grapeseed Oil or Extra virgin olive oil
- Tamari
- 1 Lemon
- Cherry Tomatoes
- Nutritional Yeast Flakes
- 1 cup raw, unsalted Cashews
- 1 Pear of choice

DIRECTIONS

Ground Cashews:

In a dry blender or food processor, place in raw cashews and blend well until a fine flour-like forms, about 20 seconds

In a large bowl, add in all ingredients except pears, ground cashews and nutritional yeast and mix well allowing the collards to fully coat, tossing about 1 minutes. Add in ground cashews and nutritional yeast then using your hands to massage salad until full coated. Toss in pears and allow to sit for 5 minutes. Breathe, Serve and Enjoy!

CREAMY DILL INFUSED POTATO SALAD

RECIPE

Servings 6 | Prep Time 25 mins | Total Time 35 mins

INGREDIENTS

- 6 medium sized Yukon gold potatoes, peeled and cut small/medium cubes
- Sea salt and pepper, to taste
- 2 celery stalks, finely diced
- 1 cup vegan mayo (Vegenaise by Follow Your Heart)
- 1 small sweet onion, finely chopped
- 1/4 cup chopped fresh dill or 1 tbsp dill powder
- 1 tbsp rice vinegar
- 1-2 tbsp yellow mustard
- 1 tsp paprika
- 1 tsp parsley

SHOPPING LIST

- 6 medium sized Yukon Gold Organic Potatoes or any Organic Potatoes
- Sea salt and Pepper
- 2 Celery Stalks
- Vegan Mayo (Vegenaise by Follow Your Heart)
- 1 Sweet Onion
- 1/4 cup fresh Dill or Dill Powder
  Rice Vinegar
  Yellow Mustard
- Paprika

DIRECTIONS

In a large pot, place potatoes in and fill with water to cover completely. Add salt and bring to a boil.

Cook until tender about 20 to 25 minutes.

Drain potatoes in a colander and set aside until warm enough to touch and cut potatoes in cubes.

Combine all the remaining ingredients in a large bowl.

Add potatoes to the bowl, tossing until full coated

Sprinkle with paprika and additional dill, salt and pepper to taste. Breathe, Serve and Enjoy!

MEGA GREEN PROTEIN

RECIPE

Servings 6 | Prep Time 10 mins | Total Time 10 mins

INGREDIENTS

- 1 bunch spinach, washed and dried
- 2 avocados, sliced
- 1 cup peas, can use frozen and allow to thaw
- 1 cup cabbage, shredded
- 2 carrots, sliced or chopped
- ½ red-onion, sliced
- 2 tomatoes, sliced or cut as desired
- 2 tbsp agave
- 2 tbsp ground flax seeds
- ½ cup extra virgin olive oil
- 2 tbsp tamari sauce
- 2 tbsp rice vinegar
- 1 lime, juice squeeze

SHOPPING LIST

- 1 bunch Spinach
- 1 bunch of Lettuce of choice
- 2 Avocados
- 1 cup Peas, can use frozen
- 1 cup Cabbage
- 2 Carrots
- 1 Red Onion
- 2 Tomatoes
- Ground Flax Seeds
- Extra virgin olive oil
- Tamari Sauce
- Agave
- Rice Vinegar
- 1 Lime

DIRECTIONS

In a small bowl, mix ground flax seeds, extra virgin olive oil, agave, tamari sauce, rice vinegar and lime juice and set aside.

In a large bowl, mix all ingredients well for about 1 minute1. Then mix in all ingredients from small bowl and continue to toss until well covered. Breathe, Serve and Enjoy!

BIG BAD BREAKFAST

RECIPE

Servings 4 | Prep Time 10 mins | Total Time 20 mins

INGREDIENTS

- 2 tbsp vegan butter
- vegan sausage patties (soy protein)
- 1 packet of extra firm tofu
- ½ cup peas (can be frozen)
- ½ cup mushrooms, sliced
- ½ onion
- 1 tbsp oregano
- 1/3 cup nutritional yeast
- ¼ cup water
- 1 tsp cumin
- 1 medium tomato, sliced
- 2 celery stalks, diced
- sprouted whole grain toast or bread of your choice
- apples, sliced

SHOPPING LIST

- Vegan Butter
- Vegan Sausage Patties (soy protein)
- 1 packet of Extra Firm Tofu
- Peas (can be frozen)
- Mushrooms
- 1 Onion
- Oregano
- Nutritional Yeast
- Cumin
- 1 medium Tomato
- 2 Celery stalks
- Sprouted Whole Grain Bread
- Apples

DIRECTIONS

Cook vegan sausage patties per package – I like to lightly fry with a little vegan butter for 2 minutes on each side then cover and allow to simmer or 2 minutes before adding in ¼ water, cover and allow to fully cook.

Drain water from tofu. Wrap tofu block in a several pieces of white paper tower or white cloth and gently squeeze out access water.

Add butter in a medium skillet to medium heat. Unwrap tofu and break in half. Using your hands, crumble one half of the tofu and then crumble in the other half of the tofu. With a wooden spoon, stir the tofu for about 2 minutes.

Add in onions, garlic, mushroom, celery, oregano, cumin and peas. Mix ingredients well allow the tofu to lightly brown. Add in peas and cook for 1 minutes. Then add nutritional yeast and water and continue stirring until all liquid has evaporated. Add additional butter to pan if tofu starts to stick heavy. Add red pepper flakes for added flavor. Serve patties, tofu scramble, sliced tomatoes over your favorite toasted bread. Breathe, Serve and Enjoy!

HEARTY BOWL OF VEGAN CHILI

RECIPE

Servings 6-8 | Prep Time 10 mins | Total Time 30 mins

INGREDIENTS

- 1 packet Beyond Meat beef crumbles (can be found in frozen section of grocer)
- 2 tbsp extra virgin extra virgin olive oil
- 1 organic onion, chopped
- 2 cubes of Edward & Sons Not Chicken Bouillon Cubes or 2 cups vegetable broth
- 2 carrots, peeled, thinly sliced
- 1 red bell pepper, seeded, chopped
- 3 large jalapeño chilies, seeded, minced (about 4 1/2 tablespoons) or red pepper flakes and Tabasco (to taste)
- 1 28-ounce can organic crushed tomatoes with added puree
- 1 can organic tomato paste
- 1/2 cup nutritional yeast flakes
- 3 cups water

SHOPPING LIST

- 1 packet Beyond Meat beef crumbles (can be found in frozen section of grocer)
- Extra Virgin Extra virgin olive oil
- 1 organic onion
- Edward & Sons Not Chicken Bullion Cubes or 2 cups Vegetable Broth
- 2 Carrots
- 1 Red Bell Pepper
- 3 large Jalapeño chilies or Red Pepper Flakes and Tabasco
- 1 28-ounce can organic Crushed Tomatoes with added puree
- 1 can organic Tomato Paste
- Nutritional Yeast flakes
- 1 15-ounce can organic Black Beans
- 1 15-ounce can organic Kidney Beans
- Rice Vinegar
- Garlic Cloves
- Chili Powder
- Ground Cumin
- Ground Coriander
- Ground Cinnamon
- Basil

- 1 15-ounce can organic black beans, rinsed, drained
- 1 15-ounce can organic kidney beans, rinsed, drained
- 2 tbsp rice vinegar
- 5 garlic cloves, minced
- 3 tbsp chili powder
- 2 tsp ground cumin
- 1 tsp ground coriander
- 1 tsp ground cinnamon
- 2 tbsp basil

DIRECTIONS - INSTANT POT

Place all ingredients in Instant Pot, select Chili (increase timer to 30 minutes). Breathe, Serve and Enjoy!

DIRECTIONS

Heat 2 tablespoons extra virgin olive oil in heavy large pot over medium-high heat. Add onions, carrots, red bell pepper, and jalapeños and sauté until onion and carrots are almost tender, about 6 minutes. Add tomatoes and tomato paste, 3 cups water, bullion (or 3 cups vegetable broth), beans, Beyond Beef, rice vinegar, garlic, and all spices. Bring to boil. Reduce heat to low, simmer and cook, covered, until mixture thickens, stirring often, about 20 minutes. Ladle chili into bowls and sprinkle with additional Nutritional Yeast Flakes. Breath, Serve and Enjoy!

OHH VEGAN CHICKEN VEGETABLE STIR FRY!

MY STORY

Feel Free to make this without the "chicken".

RECIPE

Servings 6 | Prep Time 15 mins | Total Time 30 mins

INGREDIENTS

- 1 packed soy chicken nuggets. I use Soy Delight or Beyond Meat chicken
- 1 head Broccoli, cut into florets
- 1 yellow onion, sliced
- 1 red bell pepper, diced
- 2 garlic cloves, minced
- ½ cup snow peas,
- 1 cup carrots, shredded
- 1 tbsp thyme
- 2 tbsp toasted sesame oil for sautéing
- 2 tbsp sriracha sauce
- 1 tbsp fresh ginger, minced
- 2 tbsp organic brown sugar, organic
- 1 tbsp agave, maple syrup
- 1 tbsp cornstarch or arrow root
- red pepper flakes, salt and pepper to taste

SHOPPING LIST

- 1 packet soy chicken nuggets by Soy Delight or Beyond Meat
- 1 head Broccoli, cut into florets
- 1 yellow onion, sliced
- 1 red bell pepper, diced
- 2 garlic cloves, minced
- ½ cup snow peas
- 1 cup carrots
- sesame oil
- sriracha sauce
- 1 small fresh ginger
  agave
  arrowroot or cornstarch

DIRECTIONS - SAUCE

- tamari sauce
- fresh grated ginger
- brown sugar, organic
- agave, maple syrup
- cornstarch or arrow root

SAUCE MIXTURE:

In a bowl, mix together the tamari sauce, sherry, brown sugar, arrow root or cornstarch, sriracha and ginger. Set aside.

DIRECTIONS

In a large skillet, heat the oil over medium-high heat until hot. Season the chicken lightly with salt, pepper and thyme. Add it to the skillet in a single layer and let it cook, 1 minute on each side until brown. Flip the chicken pieces and stir for 1 minute. Remove the chicken to a plate and using the excess oil/juices in the skillet.

Pour in more oil if needed and add onions, garlic and peppers and stir for about 2 minutes. Add snow peas, broccoli for stir well, cooking for 2 minutes then pour in sauce mixture.

Add chicken back to the skillet and mix together with veggies and sauce, cooking for 2 minutes more, or until the sauce is thick. Can be adjusted with 1/4 hot water and a little tamari sauce. Serve over rice or noodles. Breathe, Serve and Enjoy!

TUSCAN FOREST MUSHROOMS WITH SUN DRIED TOMATOES

RECIPE

Servings 6 | Prep Time 10 mins | Total Time 15 mins

INGREDIENTS

- 1 packet mushrooms: shiitake, cremini or Portobello, sliced
- ½ cup wild mushrooms: oyster, sliced
- 2 tbsp extra virgin extra virgin olive oil
- 1 onion, sliced
- salt and pepper
- 2 tsp thyme
- 1 tsp sage
- 1 tsp rosemary
- 1/2 tsp red pepper flakes or cayenne
- 1 tbsp tomato paste
- ½ cup sun dried tomatoes
- 1 tbsp unbleached flour
- 1 cup vegetable broth or more
- 2 tbsp vegan butter
- 3 garlic cloves, minced
- 3 tsp parsley

SHOPPING LIST

- 1 packet mushrooms: shiitake, cremini or Portobello
- ½ cup Oyster Mushrooms
- Extra Virgin Extra virgin olive oil
- 1 Onion
- Salt and Pepper
- Thyme
- Sage
- Rosemary
- Red Pepper Flakes or Cayenne
- Tomato Paste
- Sun Dried Tomatoes
- Flour or Arrow root
- Vegetable broth
- Vegan Butter
- Garlic
- Parsley

DIRECTIONS

In a large skillet, heat 2 tablespoons extra virgin olive oil over medium high heat. Add onion, garlic, salt and pepper, stirring until caramelized.

Add butter to skillet then add sun dried tomatoes and mushrooms, stir-frying for about 3 minutes. Lower heat to medium. Add thyme, sage, rosemary, red pepper and tomato paste and cook for 1 minute. Sprinkle with 1 tablespoon flour, stir to coat evenly and cook for 1 minute.

Add 1 cup of broth and stir until thickened, about 2 to 3 minute. Sauce should have gravy-like consistency. Feel free to thin out with more broth. Remove from heat and let sit 5 minutes before serving. Breathe, Serve and Enjoy! Enjoy with Quinoa, Wild or Brown Rice.

.

CREAMY HUMMUS

MY STORY

Less than 10 minutes to better than store purchased, creamy Hummus!

RECIPE

Servings 4 | Prep Time 5 mins | Total Time 10 mins

INGREDIENTS

- 1 15-ounce organic can chickpeas. Do Not drain as we will use the chickpea sauce

- 3 cloves garlic

- 1/2 cup tahini

- 2 tbsp fresh lemon juice

- ½ tsp cayenne pepper

- 1 tsp sea salt to taste

- 2 tbsp extra virgin olive oil

- 1 tsp paprika

SHOPPING LIST

- 1 15-ounce can organic chickpeas
- 3 Garlic Cloves
- Tahini
- 1 lemon to squeeze
- Cayenne Pepper
- Sea Salt
- Extra virgin olive oil
- Paprika

DIRECTIONS

In a medium size glass bowl, microwave undrained chickpeas and whole garlic cloves for 5 minutes.

Add to blender or food processor along with lemon juice, salt, cayenne pepper and tahini. Pour in extra virgin olive oil while mixing.

Continue to blend until smooth and creamy, scraping sides, taste and adjust if needed

Top with additional extra virgin olive oil and paprika and serve with organic blue chips. Breathe, Serve and Enjoy!

CURRY LENTILS & BLUE CHIPS

RECIPE

Servings 6 | Prep Time 25 mins | Total Time 1 hour

INGREDIENTS

- 1 1/4 cups lentils, rinsed
- 1/2 medium onion, diced
- 1 tbsp olive oil
- 2 medium celery stalks, diced
- 1 medium carrot, peeled, diced
- 3 medium garlic cloves, minced
- salt and pepper
- 1 tbsp oregano
- 1 tsp cumin
- 1 tsp curry powder
- 1 quart vegetable broth
- 1 bay leaf
- 1/4 tsp thyme
- 1 tsp rice vinegar or sherry vinegar
- organic blue chips

SHOPPING LIST

- Lentils
- 1 medium onion
- Extra Virgin Olive Oil
- 2 medium Celery stalks
- 1 medium Carrot
- Garlic Cloves
- Salt and Pepper
- Oregano
- Cumin
- Curry Powder
- 1 quart vegetable broth
- 1 bay leaf
- 1/4 tsp thyme
- 1 tsp rice vinegar or sherry vinegar
- organic blue chips

DIRECTIONS

Heat the oil in a large saucepan over medium heat. Add the celery, carrot, and onion and cook, stirring occasionally, until softened. Stir in the garlic and cook or 1 minute. Add pinches of salt and pepper.

Then add broth, lentils, bay leaf, thyme, curry, oregano, cumin, pepper and stir to combine. Cover and bring to a simmer, about 15 minutes.

Once simmering, reduce the heat to low and continue simmering, covered, until the lentils and vegetables are soft, about 20 minutes more.

Taste and season with more salt or pepper as needed, then stir in the vinegar. Top with organic blue chips. Breathe, Serve and Enjoy!

OHH MY... CAULIFLOWER RICE

MY STORY

Eat this alone or add to any of your favorite entrees to substitute rice.

RECIPE

Servings 6 | Prep Time 5 mins | Total Time 10 mins

INGREDIENTS

- 1 large cauliflower, washed, dried and cut into four pieces

- 1 lime, sliced

- 2 tbsp cilantro

- 1 tbsp vegan butter

- salt and pepper to taste

SHOPPING LIST

- 1 large cauliflower
- 1 lime
- Cilantro
- Vegan Butter
- Salt and Pepper

DIRECTIONS

Use a medium sized hole grater to grate cauliflower into the size of rice. Ok to include large stubborn pieces

Transfer to a clean towel or paper towel and press to remove any excess moisture

In a large skillet, sauté cauliflower over medium heat with 1 tbsp vegan butter. Cover with a lid for tenderness and cook for a total of 4 – 7 minutes then season with cilantro, squeeze lime and add sliced limes with salt and pepper to taste. Breathe, Serve and Enjoy!

YES TO EDAMAME DUMPLINGS!

RECIPE

Servings 4 | Prep Time 15 mins | Total Time 15 mins

INGREDIENTS

- 1 package of frozen edamame, shelled
- 1 package or 20 vegan wonton wrappers
- 2 tbsp green onions, chopped
- 2 tbsp tamari sauce
- 1 tsp agave
- 1 tbsp lemon juice
- 1 tsp sesame oil
- 1 tsp ground cumin
- 1/4 tsp sea salt
- 1/2 tsp red pepper flakes
- 3 garlic cloves, minced
- 1 tsp ginger powder
- 1/2 cup water

SHOPPING LIST

- 1 package of frozen Edamame, shelled
- I package or about 20 vegan Wonton Wrappers
- Green Onions
- Tamari Sauce
- Agave
- Lemon Juice or 1 Lemon
- Sesame Oil
- Ground Cumin
- Sea Salt
- Red Pepper Flakes
- Garlic cloves
- Ginger Powder

DIRECTIONS

Sauce: Whisk tamari sauce and agave and half of the red pepper flakes ingredients in a small bowl.

Dumplings: cook edamame per directions then rinse with cold water and drain. Combine edamame, green onions, garlic, ginger, lemon juice, sesame oil, cumin, red pepper flakes, garlic, and salt in a food processor until smooth.

Working with 1 wonton wrapper at a time, cover remaining wrappers with a damp towel to prevent drying, spoon about 1 teaspoon edamame mixture in center of each wrapper. Moisten edges of dough with water; fold opposite corners to form a triangle then bend to meet ends, pinching points to seal. Place dumplings in a steamer (I used a wooded bamboo steamer) working in batches if needed, cover and steam until wrappers have softened and filling is cooked through, about 7 minutes.

GARLIC SPINACH, SAUTEED

RECIPE

Servings 4 | Prep Time 5 mins | Total Time 15 mins

INGREDIENTS

- 2 bunches spinach
- 1/2 sweet onion, sliced
- 4 garlic cloves, minced
- 1 tbsp grapeseed oil
- ¼ cup red bell pepper
- 1/4 cup red yellow pepper
- 1 tsp thyme
- salt and pepper to taste

SHOPPING LIST

- 2 bunches Spinach
- 1 Sweet Onion
- Garlic Cloves
- Grapeseed oil
- Red Bell Pepper
- Yellow Bell Pepper
- Thyme
- Salt and Pepper

DIRECTIONS

In a hot skillet, add oil and all above ingredients. Cook until Spinach has fully wilted. Pour Spinach on a plate along with spinach juice. Breathe, Serve and Enjoy!

VEGEN CHICKEN NOODLE SOUP

RECIPE

Servings 6 | Prep Time 10 mins | Total Time 25 mins

INGREDIENTS

- 1 package vegan chicken, cut into chucks (Beyond Meat, Garden) are good choices

- 2 carrots, diced

- ½ cup yellow bell pepper, diced

- 2 tbsp extra virgin olive oil1

- 1 small onion, diced

- 2 garlic cloves, minced

- 2 celery stalks, diced

- ½ tsp sage

- 1 tsp oregano

- 2 bullion, no chicken bullion or 4-5 cups vegetable broth

- 1 ½ cup pasta noodles. I used rice pasta shells

- 1 bay leaf

- 1 tbsp Italian seasoning

- pepper to taste

SHOPPING LIST

- Vegan Chicken (Beyond Meat or Gardein)
- 2 Carrots
- 1 Yellow Bell Pepper
- Extra Virgin Olive Oil
- 1 Onion
- Garlic
- Celery
- Oregano
- Sage
- Bullion: No chicken bullion or 1 quart Vegetable Broth
- Pasta Noodles
- Bay Leaf
- Italian Seasoning
- Pepper

DIRECTIONS

In a large pot over medium heat, add oil and chopped chicken pieces and oregano. Stir and allow chicken to lightly brown then remove chicken from pot. Add more oil to pot along with onion, celery, carrots, garlic and bell pepper. Cook until just tender.

Add the vegetable broth, seasoned chicken and noodles and bring to a boil. Reduce heat and add in sage, bay leaf and Italian seasoning and allow to cook for 15 minutes.

Breathe, Serve and Enjoy!

GINGER LEMON APPLE PINEAPPLE BLAST

RECIPE

Servings 2 | Prep Time 5 | Total Time 10

INGREDIENTS

- 1 lemon, peeled
- 2 apples, your choice
- ½ cup pineapples (can be frozen)
- 1/2 to 1 habanero
- 3 inches fresh ginger
- 3 inches fresh turmeric root or 1/2 tsp turmeric powder
- 1 cucumber, cut
- 1 bunch celery
- 1 bunch cilantro
- 1 bunch parsley
- 1 handful fresh mint

SHOPPING LIST

- 1 lemon
- 2 apples, your choice
- ½ cup pineapples (can be frozen)
- 1 habanero
- 3 inches fresh ginger
- fresh turmeric root or 1/2 tsp turmeric powder
- 1 cucumber
- 1 bunch celery
- 1 bunch cilantro
- 1 bunch parsley
- 1 handful fresh mint

DIRECTIONS

Juice all ingredients

Cut final juice amount with 1/3 water

Add filtered water or ice if a blender is used instead of a juicer

THE SALAD

RECIPE

Servings 4 | Prep Time 10 mins | Total Time 10 mins

INGREDIENTS

- 2 cups mixed greens
- 1 can garbanzo beans, organic, drained and rinsed
- 1 red bell pepper, chopped
- 1 red yellow pepper, chopped
- 1 medium tomatoes or a handful of cherry tomatoes, diced
- ½ tsp cayenne pepper
- 1 tsp oregano
- 2 tbsp tahini
- 1 tsp agave
- 2 tbsp rice vinegar
- 1 small sweet onion, diced
- 2 garlic cloves, minced
- ¼ cup parsley, chopped
- salt and pepper to taste

SHOPPING LIST

- 2 cups mixed greens
- 1 can garbanzo beans, organic
- 1 red bell pepper
- 1 red yellow pepper
- 1 Tomato or a handful of Cherry Tomatoes
- Cayenne Pepper
- Oregano
- Tahini
- Agave
- Rice Vinegar
- 1 small sweet Onion
- Garlic Cloves
- Parsley
- Salt and Pepper

DIRECTIONS

In a large bowl, place garbanzo beans in along with rice vinegar, tahini, oregano, agave, salt and pepper to taste and stir to coat evenly. Mix in all remaining ingredients well. Breathe, Serve and Enjoy!

No need for salad dressing as the juices from the garbanzo beans and veggies will be succulent. Breathe, Serve and Enjoy!

TOFU SCRAMBLE TACOS

RECIPE

Servings 4 | Prep Time 10 mins | Total Time 20 mins

INGREDIENTS

- 1 package organic tofu, drained and dried
- ¼ cup mushrooms, sliced
- ½ cup onions, sliced
- 1/2 red bell peppers, diced
- 1/2 cup nutritional yeast
- 2 tsp garlic powder
- 1 jalapeno pepper, chopped
- 1 tsp cumin
- 1/2 tsp turmeric
- 1 tsp oregano
- 1 tbsp grapeseed or extra virgin oil
- salt and pepper
- Warm tortillas
- 2 avocados, sliced

SHOPPING LIST

- 1 package organic Tofu
- Mushrooms
- 1 Onion
- 1 Red Bell Peppers
- Nutritional Yeast
- Garlic Powder
- Jalapeno Pepper
- Cumin
- Turmeric
- Oregano
- Grapeseed or Extra Virgin Olive Oil
- Warm Tortillas
- Avocados

DIRECTIONS

Crumble tofu into a medium bowl. Toss with all spices, coating well. Add in the oil and continue to toss.

Add the tofu into a hot skillet. Cook and with a wooden spoon stir until tofu is golden brown, dark around edges. Wrap in warm tortillas and serve with avocados. Breathe, Serve and Enjoy!

VEGAN PO BOY – OHH BOY!

RECIPE

Servings 4 | Prep Time 15 mins| Total Time 40 mins

INGREDIENTS

- Oyster Marinade:
- About 20 pieces of oyster mushrooms
- 2 tbsp ground flax
- 6 tbsp water
- 1 cup non-dairy milk of choice
- 1/4 cup rice vinegar
- 2 tbsp vegan Worcestershire sauce
- 2 tsp garlic powder
- 2 tsp dried thyme
- salt and pepper to taste
- 1 1/2 - 2 vegetable oil

MUSHROOM BREAD COATING

- 1/2 cup panko bread crumbs
- 1/4 cup corn meal
- 1/4 cup all-purpose flour (rice, garbanzo, your choice)
- 1 tsp cayenne
- 1 tsp garlic powder

SHOPPING LIST

- Oyster Marinade:
- About 20 pieces of Oyster Mushrooms
- Ground Flax
- Non-Dairy Milk of choice
- Rice Vinegar
- Vegan Worcestershire Sauce
- Garlic Powder
- Dried Thyme
- Salt and Pepper
- Vegetable Oil
- Mushroom Bread Coating:
- 1/2 cup panko bread crumbs
- 1/4 cup corn meal
- 1/4 cup all-purpose flour (rice, garbanzo, your choice)
- 1 tsp cayenne
- 1 tsp garlic powder
- 1 tsp dried thyme
- 1 tsp paprika
- salt and pepper
- 1 medium onion, sliced
- rolls of choice

- 1 tsp dried thyme
- 1 tsp paprika
- salt and pepper
- 1 medium onion, sliced
- rolls of choice

DIRECTIONS

Mix together ground flax and water and place in the refrigerator for about 10 minutes to thicken.

Mix together non-dairy milk, rice vinegar, Worcestershire, garlic powder, thyme and white pepper. Add flax mixture once thickened and pour marinade over pieces of mushrooms in a large zipper. Coat evenly

In the interim, mix together the breading ingredients and set aside

In a heavy skillet on medium to high heat, add 2 tablespoons of oil then add onions and allow to caramelize. Remove onion from oil and place on a paper towel. Add additional oil for frying mushrooms.

Piece by piece, add mushrooms from the marinade and place directly in the bread coating evenly on all sides using your hands. Place each piece into the hot oil and fry for 2-3 minutes, flipping half way through.

With a tong, place mushrooms onto a paper towel to absorb excess oil. Continue to bread the mushrooms, frying in small batches.

Cut rolls in half, add in mushrooms and top with caramelized onions and add your favorite sauce. I used this sauce: Not pictured:

- 1/2 cup vegan mayo
- 1 tbsp tabasco sauce

- 1 tbsp sweet green relish
- 1 tbsp pickle juice

Breathe, Serve and Enjoy!

VEGAN MAC & CHEESE – OHH SO GOOD!

RECIPE

Servings 6-8 | Prep Time 15 mins | Total Time 40

INGREDIENTS

- 3 medium potatoes, peeled and chopped
- 3 carrots, peeled and chopped
- 2 cup water used to boil potatoes
- 1/4 cup nutritional yeast flakes
- 2 tbsp lemon juice
- 1 tsp apple cider vinegar
- ¼ cup soy or coconut milk
- 1 tsp salt
- a couple dashes of tabasco sauce
- 1 tsp onion powder
- 1 tsp garlic powder
- 1 tsp mustard
- 1 tsp turmeric
- ½ paprika
- 2 cups elbow pasta: quinoa, rice, whole wheat, gluten free or your choice

SHOPPING LIST

- 3 medium Potatoes
- 3 Carrots
- Nutritional Yeast Flakes
- 1 Lemon
- Apple Cider Vinegar
- Soy or Coconut milk
- Salt and Pepper
- Tabasco Sauce
- Onion Powder
- Garlic Powder
- Mustard
- Turmeric
- Paprika
- 2 cups Elbow Pasta: quinoa, rice, whole wheat, gluten free or your choice

DIRECTIONS

Cook macaroni per package, drain and set aside.

Bring several cups of water to boil in a pot. Place potatoes and carrots in the boiling water and cook for about 10 minutes or until vegetables are soft enough to blend.

Place veggies in blender and add ¾ cup of cooking water to your blender, along with all remaining ingredients, except paprika and bread crumbs.

Blend until smooth.

Pour sauce over your cooked macaroni, taste for salt and place macaroni mixture in a baking dish, sprinkle with bread crumbs and paprika and bake at 350 degrees for 25 minutes or until crumbs are turning golden brown.

Breathe, Serve and Enjoy!

CORN AND TOMATO BRUSCHETTA

RECIPE

Servings 6 pieces | Prep Time 10 mins | Total Time 15 mins

INGREDIENTS

- 4 medium ripe tomatoes
- 1 small red onion
- 1 medium jalapeno
- 2 tablespoons extra virgin olive oil
- 2 tbsp basil
- ½ tsp paprika
- 1 lime for juice
- 2 garlic cloves, chopped
- Salt and pepper
- Six 1/2-inch thick slices vegan French bread or Italian

SHOPPING LIST

- 4 medium ripe Tomatoes
- 1 small Red Onion
- 1 medium Jalapeno
- Extra Virgin Olive Oil
- Basil
- Paprika
- 1 Lime for juice
- Garlic cloves
- Salt and pepper
- Six 1/2-inch thick slices vegan French bread or Italian

DIRECTIONS

In a skillet on medium to high heat, stir in corn for 1 minute. Remove from heat. Sprinkle with salt and pepper and remove from heat.

Brush bread with olive oil and broil on low each side until crisp. Remove from heat.

Core tomatoes and cut in half. Spoon out juices and seeds and dice tomatoes. Add them to corn and mix in garlic, jalapeno peppers, onions, lime juice, basil, paprika and 1 tablespoon oil. Season to taste with salt and pepper.

Breathe, Serve and Enjoy with grilled bread!

AVOCADO TOAST

MY STORY

Bring on the avocados, the healthy monounsaturated fat, that helps lower bad cholesterol and certainly a good source of fiber

RECIPE

Servings 4 | Prep Time 5 mins | Total Time 10 mins

INGREDIENTS

- 2 whole fresh avocados
- ½ cup cherry tomatoes
- ½ tsp sea salt
- 1 jalapeno pepper
- 1 tsp raw coconut vinegar
- ½ tsp garlic powder
- 2 tbsp cilantro
- ¼ tsp black pepper
- Toasted bread

SHOPPING LIST

- 2 whole fresh Avocados
- Cherry tomatoes
- Sea salt
- 1 Jalapeno Pepper
- Raw Coconut Vinegar or Rice Vinegar
- Garlic Powder
- Cilantro
- Salt and Pepper

DIRECTIONS

In a medium bowl, mix all ingredients, mashing avocados well. Clean, cut open, put in a bowl and Mash avocados.

Spoon on toasted bread and top with sliced cherry tomatoes.

Breathe, Serve and Enjoy!

ABOUT THE AUTHOR

I believe that:

Food can be incredibly healing

Eating healthy plant based food can be easy to cook and most importantly, Ohhlicious!

Health imbalances within the body are a wake-up call that can positively change your life if you choose to listen

MICHELLE
VEGAN CHEF

Michelle cooks every meal as if it were to nurture her own body and soul. Her love affair with cooking began at the age of 9 growing up in public housing in Washington, DC. just walking distance from the White House, watching her grandmother, Gussie cook. It was a daily routine for Michelle as she was often left to complete meals started by her grandmother Gussie, her food mentor. She mastered to perfection with proper in the kitchen training while living in DC, Atlanta, NY and SC. Eight years later she embraces her love for vegan cooking with creativity, passion, healing and love.

Throughout the years she has developed skillful techniques, including working with world-renowned Raw Vegan, Lou Corona. Her wide experience in balancing flavor, texture and healthy eating brings the best of all cultures to the table. As a conscious eater herself she is a wellness enthusiast with the purpose of inspiring people to eat healthy and see food as a source of nourishment and every meal as a ritual celebrating your body. What helped Michelle evolve from eating animal based foods to a seasoned vegan is her knowledge and affinity for health, food ingredients, along with her ability to uncover flavors that mimics her Grandmother's cooking without compromising taste!

Michelle suffered a lifetime of chronic lung disease until she took her health in her own hands. In 2009 while on a family vacation flight to San Diego, she read a book that changed her life. Michelle entered the plane an omnivore and exited a vegan; three months later she was no longer dependent on prescription asthma medications. Through embracing a 100% whole foods plant based diet, she healed herself through reversing asthma of what doctors insisted was an incurable ailment. During that journey the vision to share and help others through her experiences and education was realized.

Along the way, she learned about factory farming, confirming her decision to become vegan. She also learned that vegan food needed not only be good for the body but also taste great or no one was going to eat it! Michelle earned her undergraduate degree from Washington Adventist University, did her graduate studies at the University of Maryland University College and worked in legal administration, executive sales & training capacities for years in Corporate America before leaving to fully embrace her healing and passion of being a beacon of hope. At 51 and a Certified Integrative Health Coach, she is Founder of Ohh Michelle, LLC, a company dedicated to empowering people to reconnect with their body, mind, and soul through food/nutrition, yoga and wellness. She has co-authored a couple Amazon Bestselling books, including her 1st inspirational book, *Ohhmazing Wellness: Shift Your Vision and Create the Healthy and Happy Life You Deserve*. She has also studied under the Institute of Integrative Nutrition and Cornell University's Plant Based Nutrition program. Michelle is a Yoga Teacher and facilitates Corporate Wellness events, including being a facilitator for Canyon Ranch Institute. Mostly, Michelle loves good food and loves sharing it with others. Be part of the movement and be inspired, encouraged, motivated to learn about food that's good for your soul.

One Love Many Hugs,

Michelle Grandy

Join us today at www.ohhliciousfood.com/thebook

79905379R00150

Made in the USA
Lexington, KY
26 January 2018